SALLY BAYLE   Royal Literary
Fund Fellow.   l responses to
literature, inc... ... ... study of Sylvia Plath's
relationship to the visual arts, *Eye Rhymes*, and a study of Plath
as a cultural icon, *Representing Sylvia Plath*. In 2010 she
completed a cross-media study of Emily Dickinson as a way
of thinking about America's relationship to space and place,
Home on the Horizon. She is the author of *The Private Life of
the Diary*.

'Extraordinary … an astonishing tale, astonishingly written in
clear, precise prose … Bayley is exceptionally good at bringing
us into the child's world … there's a raw, visceral power to the
writing, which turns the abstract physical on almost every
page'   CHRISTINA PATTERSON, *Sunday Times*

'A beguiling, eccentric, funny memoir'

NINA STIBBE, *Observer*

'Her bold poetic prose carries the sinister cackle of Bertha
Mason on a warm breeze through St Mary Mead, to be wafted
away in comic disdain by Betsey Trotwood … I loved Bayley's
memoir'   HELEN BROWN, *Daily Telegraph*

'Just let its poetic rhythms lap over you … it left me longing
for more of Bayley's recollections from a place of relative
tranquillity'   LUCY MANGAN, *Spectator*

'Thanks to the guidance of three beloved fictional characters ... who came alive in her imagination, young Sally negotiated her way through the jungle of her childhood ... what this book proves is how a child starved of stability can find it and be saved by good books ... [A] resolutely cheerful memoir'

YSENDA MAXTONE GRAHAM, *The Times*

'Bayley's family are compelling, certainly, but it's the formidable and moving lines of much-loved prose, sketched long ago in the classics, that provide much of *Girl With Dove*'s horsepower'

TANYA SWEENEY, *Irish Times*

'[Bayley's] childhood books are brought vividly to life, as are the remembered pleasures of first encountering them'

HARRIET BAKER, *Times Literary Supplement*

'Excellently written ... a very enjoyable book, particularly for those of us who love a good mystery'

ANGIE JOHNSON, *Oxford Times*

'Shot through with deliciously quirky humour, *Girl With Dove* is a testament to innocence, resilience and the protective power of the imagination ... This is a story about the child's need to make sense of chaos and the redemptive power of stories to bestow meaning ... The word "mesmerising" is frequently applied to memoirs, but seldom as deservedly as in the case of *Girl With Dove*'

REBECCA ABRAMS, *Financial Times*

'Be warned: here be dragons. *Girl With Dove* flies off the map. Charting the odyssey of its bibliophilic heroine's imagination, it treats us to age-old bildungsroman pleasures. Bittersweet, tragicomic terrain, with flashes of the familiar and the universal against the quirky, murky landscape of this girl's singular childhood. But *Girl With Dove* is more than a memoir: a detective story, a mystery, a magical and strange genealogy. Darkly enthralling and yet sparkling, painful and yet funny, this book is dizzyingly many things at once'

ANDREA ASHWORTH, author of *Once in a House on Fire*

'What an astonishing, funny, shocking and inventive book. Sally Bayley is an extraordinarily clever and versatile writer. Thoroughly enjoyable' ALEXANDER MASTERS, author of *Stuart* and *A Life Discarded*

'Into the burgeoning genre of writing about the power of books to shape our lives comes a wholly new and mesmerising voice: Sally Bayley writes through the eyes of a child living a very strange childhood as convincingly as the Dickens of *David Copperfield*' JONATHAN BATE, author of *Ted Hughes*

'A dark, funny, heartbreaking memoir which celebrates the power of literature to transform, inform and comfort'

ALICE JOLLY, author of *Dead Babies and Seaside Towns*, winner of the Ackerley Prize 2016

GIRL WITH DOVE

DOVE

A LIFE BUILT BY BOOKS

SALLY BAYLEY

WILLIAM
COLLINS

William Collins
An imprint of HarperCollins*Publishers*
1 London Bridge Street
London SE1 9GF

www.WilliamCollinsBooks.com

First published in Great Britain by William Collins in 2018
This William Collins paperback edition published in 2019

1

A catalogue record for this book is
available from the British Library

ISBN 978-0-00-822689-3

Printed and bound in Great Britain by
CPI Group (UK) Ltd, Croydon

For Angela Christine Bayley,
Soul of a Rose

'Attention, taken to its highest degree, is the same thing as prayer. It presupposes faith and love. Absolutely unmixed attention is prayer.'

Simone Weil, *Gravity and Grace* (English edition, 1952, translated by Emma Crawford and Mario von der Ruhr)

CONTENTS

PART THREE

Preface

THE READER'S BACKSTORY

All stories have backstories, at least all stories worth knowing about, and all readers want to pry into those unlit spaces. We read to get back to those dark and dusty corners, to scrape back to old patterns: the strange symbol beneath the damp plaster, the squiggles on the crumbling wall. Reading is a strong torch shining through the dark.

As a child I was terrified of the story of Sleeping Beauty and the jealous old fairy who stalks the palace grounds. The fairy is furious that someone so enchanting should live, so she casts a spell on Beauty. Soon after, Beauty pricks her finger on a spindle; the needle is so sharp, and cuts so deep, that everyone is sure Beauty will bleed to death.

But another, kinder, fairy turns back the spell so that Beauty will not die, but instead sleeps for a hundred years. Everyone agrees that this is better than nothing: sleeping is better than dying. But from that day on, the king and queen begin to watch their daughter and worry. Not a day goes by that they don't think of that sharp needle cutting through their fair daughter's skin.

———————————

Reading is a form of escape, and an avid reader is an escape artist. I began my escape the moment I started to read. Aged four, I already had sentences stored up; I knew some words and I could put them together in a line.

But Mum didn't have enough time to help me. She was managing babies and nappies; she was turning dingy cotton nappies from grey to white. Back from grey to white, sparkling white.

But white is very hard to get back once it's been *ruined*. Mum used that word a lot. To *ruin* something was to turn it from white to grey. Nappies were never completely ruined, because you could boil them and bring them back to life. Nappies could always start again, as long as you kept them on the boil for long enough and didn't mind the steam.

Mum hated plastic on babies' bottoms. She preferred cotton, and cotton needed cooking to make it clean.

Every day Mummy boiled the nappies inside a large grey saucepan that sat on the hob. I climbed on a stool and peered down into the grey water. I stirred the nappies with a wooden spoon, and I was the Nappy Witch.

Mummy took out the nappies and hung them on the backline. They flapped in the breeze. I ran underneath them, and when they touched my scalp I screamed. Nappies were hard and scratchy. I asked Mummy why nappies weren't soft, and she said they had to be strong so they could take all that *scalding* hot water.

'But why do you boil them so much, Mummy? You're making them hard.'

'You can't have those nasty plastic things so close to a baby's bottom. Cotton is what you should put next to a baby's bottom, nice strong cotton.'

Strong cotton, strong cotton, strong cotton. Strong cotton. I sat beneath Strong Cotton and I felt my brother's fingers and toes. Strong cotton kept out the sky, strong cotton kept the wind away. Strong cotton kept babies nice and safe.

I made a tent from strong cotton and put my baby brother David in it. David was Baby Jesus and I was Mary, which, by the way, is my middle name.

'Where on earth have you put the baby?' Mummy asked. 'Stop playing silly devils.' Her face was hot and red and the clouds were poking up from behind.

'He's here, Mummy. He's asleep, beneath the strong cotton.'

'I can see that, young lady, I'm not blind. Stop playing silly devils with the baby. Leave him there under the tree, near the roses, where I told you. I want him out where I can see him.'

Mummy stuck her nose in the air and went back into the kitchen.

Then one day David went missing. I couldn't find him anywhere. He was no longer beneath the roses when I went out after lunch. I put my hand inside his cot and felt soft white cotton on my hands, bare white cotton, warm cotton, and I yelled,

'Mummy, Mummy, David's not here! Mummy, Mummy, David's not here! Mummy, Mummy, where is David, Mummy, where is David?'

Sometime in the summer of 1976, the very hot summer, the summer we were all dripping-hot and cross, the Nappy Witch came and took David away, and Mummy went to bed for a very long time. She went for two hundred sleeps, maybe more. Soon after, the Lady Upstairs moved in and Mummy fell under a thick, dark spell. She didn't wake for years.

PART ONE

I

MISS MARPLE

Miss Marple was at the back of her garden wrestling with her roses when Dolly Bantry called by. The greenfly had got to them again and she was determined to see them off. Dolly would just have to wait for her tea! Miss Marple gave a vigorous spray from her bottle of lemon-scented chemicals. She shook the pink petals ever so gently and untied her garden apron. She rubbed her hands and gave one of her small, barely noticeable smiles.

(Miss Marple by me, age eight)

When I was eight I wanted to be Miss Marple. I still do. Miss Marple knows everything about everyone, but nobody knows anything about her. She has no backstory. You can't see behind her and you can never get around her. Miss Marple sits in her chair in the front of St Mary Mead and looks out upon the world. There is nothing behind that antique chair except china shepherdesses and fallen roses.

When I think of Miss Marple I always think of my mother and grandmother and their old English roses. That is Mum spraying off the greenfly at the back of the garden. That is my grandmother putting on the kettle for tea, my grandmother, Edna May, with her nose against the window, watching Mum snip the blooms. Tea roses, climbers, I don't know which, but pale pink, baby pink, the pink of Mum's pillowcases; the pink of Little Bo Peep's cheeks when she blushes from the heat.

'Sit in the shade,' Mum says. 'Always sit in the shade, never on the side of a hill. Wherever you are, find a nice bit of shade. English girls shouldn't sit out in the sun. Cover yourself up and put on a nice hat with a wide brim.' Pink, rose pink, the colour of my straw hat, after all these years.

I know the names of all the old English flowers because I had a grandmother and a mother who tended to them at the bottom of our scrubby patch of garden. I am the daughter of an English florist and I have been trained to smell flowers suspiciously. If the roses didn't smell, they weren't real.

'Artificial!' Mum declared. 'Nothing at all. Not a single bit. Not even a tiny bit of pong!'

Roses that don't pong weren't roses at all. When you smelled a rose you had to make sure that what you were smelling was the real thing, the old English thing, the smell that sent you back. Ring-a-ring-of-roses, a pocket full of posies, we all fall down, and back, headlong back.

English flowers should always send you back, back to days when girls wore aprons to do their chores and nannies fussed over tea and scones in the nursery. Days that never existed, days that never were, days we dreamed up from storybooks and nursery rhymes. But we wanted them nonetheless: as much as my mother wanted her roses to grow up alongside the wall and behave nicely; as much as Miss Jane Marple wanted to defeat the greenfly so that she could tell Dolly Bantry before tea that she had won, and that her roses were now as bona fide and factual as the Bayeux Tapestry.

———

Miss Marple likes to deal with facts, because facts are concrete. Mum likes facts too. Facts are as square as her windowboxes filled with pansies.

'You've got to get your facts straight, Sally. First ask, what are the facts? You've got to get your facts first before you can begin anything!'

But if you want facts you have to go looking for them. 'They won't come to you,' Mum says. 'You have to make an effort!'

Miss Marple finds most of her facts inside St Mary Mead, the quiet English village she has lived in all her life. She knows everything she needs lies inside that quaint, chocolate-box place. Open up the lid, and there she is: an old lady tucked inside a pretty village. St Mary Mead with its Norman church spire and neat borders, St Mary Mead with its pleasant-faced locals, St Mary Mead full of people who remind you of someone else.

'It reminds me of Mr Hargreaves up at the Mount,' Miss Marple tells her nephew, Raymond, when he comes looking for facts for his novel. But Raymond doesn't follow, because between you and me, Raymond isn't half as clever as he thinks he is.

He doesn't know that you don't have to go very far to find a fact. Miss Marple knows that facts can be found by looking just over there: in the face of your mother as she lifts her head from the hot pan; in the veins of your grandmother's hands as she picks up the shopping from the stairs; in the pattern on the curtains you stared at as a child.

> There were small gay papier-mache tables in the drawing
> room, inlaid with mother-of-pearl and painted with castles
> and roses … for curtains, Gwenda had chosen old
> fashioned chintz of pale egg-shell blue with prim urns of
> roses and yellow birds on them.
>
> (Agatha Christie, *Sleeping Murder*)

———

As a child I was terrified of curtains. Flapping curtains were big black birds out to get me. Curtains were black-winged creatures that came in the night and covered my face. Curtains hid spiders and flies. Curtains suffocated sleepless children.

People hide behind curtains. In English villages, women spy behind their net curtains. 'Net curtains cover a multitude of sins,' Mum used to say. 'You can get away with murder if you hang your curtains well.' You can watch the world go by and no one will ever know that you are snooping and sneaking.

My mother loved her net curtains. She hated it when they started to get dingy and dirty, when The Woman Upstairs moved in and brought her yellow clouds of smoke.

But this came later. Before then, there were no net curtains in our downstairs flat, only a scrappy back door that flapped open whenever *the sea is blowing a sharp wind across the front*, my grandmother said. My grandmother, Maisie – Maze; my grandmother, who had knobbly fingers from arthritis and who never owned a smart handbag like Miss Marple because she didn't have the time to clutch it tight with two hands. My grandmother, who never had two hands spare because her hands were always in soapy water, in the sink, or under the grill; my grandmother pulling out rows of toasted cheese or dragging a bicycle basket full of bread up the stairs.

But sometimes my grandmother went into the garden and snapped the heads of peas. She rarely did the roses. Those were for Mum. No. Maisie did the vegetables and peas, the beans and potatoes, the cabbages and rhubarb. My grandmother was like Mr McGregor: she dug her spade deep down inside the soil until she made the worms scream.

2

GRANDMOTHERS

In 1976, when I was four, the water ran out. There were no more baths. Worse than that, Mum's roses were wilting. She rushed back and forth through the back door with perfume bottles filled with water. Mum spent all summer spraying her roses back to life.

'That way the police won't know,' she told Maze. 'They won't come snooping about. As long as I don't get the hose-pipe out, nothing will look amiss. A few drops of water here or there isn't going to make much difference. I must keep them moist, I must keep the roots moist, Maze, twice a day, morning and night. They don't stand a chance in this heat. They'll be killed off. I don't want my roses killed off after all this.'

After all this. Mum said this a lot. *After all this* was Mum's effort to plant her roses against a crumbling brick wall, to turn *a nasty bit of council turf* into Miss Marple's garden. *After all this* was something grown-ups said about things that happened before us, before my brothers or I were born, before we even arrived at our house by the sea. After all this was *back then*, back when things were different, *quite* different, Mum said.

After all this meant that I had a grandmother who lived with us. Maisie was Edna May, but we called her Maze and she was with us ever since I can remember. Maze was before and after all this; Maze was always and everything. Maisie, Maze, Edna May Turner, the old lady whose back bent like a turtle; the little old lady who rode her bike along the sea front in a gale-force wind. Maze, the lady who picked us up from school when Mum wasn't well. Maze, Maisie, Mary, May, Mary Mary, quite contrary, how does your garden grow? *Like this, just like this!*

Maze, Maisie, Mary, May. Finding out adults' real names is difficult. Everyone is in disguise. Miss Marple is usually 'Miss Marple' but sometimes she is 'Jane Marple', like Jane in the Peter and Jane books we read at school. I don't know any other Janes, not J-A-N-E Janes anyway. But it's hard to imagine Miss Marple as a little girl like Jane, with yellow hair and a white cardigan, who plays with her blue rubber ball in the garden.

Jane is a Christian name, which means it comes first. Adults call you by your Christian name and so do your friends. Jane has yellow hair and her skin is brown because she spends all her time outside. Jane is always throwing a ball into the air, or chasing her dog, or running after her brother, Peter. Jane doesn't look as though she ever sits down and reads a book. Jane plays in the garden in her pretty pink dress and nice white cardigan. Jane looks happy doing this.

In the Peter and Jane books Jane isn't reading, but I wasn't reading before I went to school. Mummy didn't have time. She said she was very sorry but she couldn't sit down with me and read a book right now *because she had to put the nappies on*. School would do that for me and I would be all the better for waiting my dear.

When I first discovered words they were sitting with their arms folded nicely on small squares of white card: 'pretty', 'nice', 'much', 'like', 'but', 'of', 'is', 'ball', 'play', 'jump', 'dog', 'outside'. The words were all about Peter and Jane and Peter and Jane only ever did one or two things. Peter and Jane played with their dog or they played with their ball in the garden. When Peter and Jane were outside playing the sun was always shining. Sometimes they got hot. Then Jane took off her white crochet cardigan (crow-sh-ay) and put it on the back steps. Her mum got cross when she did that because she'd only just washed it and dirt stains never came out of white. Not properly.

Peter and Jane are always playing and they are always happy. They are never at school and they are never reading. I don't know why, because reading is the most important thing. Reading, my grandmother told me, was *the stepping stone to better things*. If you were a good reader you would never have to face *all this*. You would never have to crawl over the big grey rock at the bottom of the garden with the sharp edges that stubbed your toes. You would never have to make a garden from scratch. You would never have to borrow a drill from the council and pull up all the muck someone else had left behind. You would never have to work for the council. You would *never ever* have to take the bins out.

———————————

It was my grandmother who first helped me read, my grand-mother, Edna May Turner. When she was young, Edna May was like one of Miss Marple's girls. She was a girl who came to polish silver and serve tea on the lawn; a girl who came to shine up the oak banister; a girl to make gooseberry fool and collect the windfall apples in the autumn; a girl to answer the doorbell; a girl to run errands in the village.

In 1930 or thereabouts (what year was my grandmother born?) Edna May Turner was carrying out the tea; she was crossing a hot lawn in a pretty English village. Edna May, the maid who was coming on nicely; Edna, the maid Miss Marple had found through her friend Dolly Bantry, was carrying a silver teapot towards an old lady sitting in the shade. Edna was concentrating so hard on the tray in front of her that she couldn't see that the woman in front of her was lifting a large pink bloom towards her companion.

———————————

Miss Marple is a white-haired old lady with a gentle, appealing manner.

(*The Murder at the Vicarage*)

How old is Miss Marple? Nobody knows. My grandmother was in her sixties and then her seventies when she was living with us, but we never really thought about how old she was. Grandmothers are just there, always and forever. They never go away and they never get older. Grandmothers are like the stone lion that sits on the corner of our front steps. Maze sits on her kitchen stool and slowly grows green lichen around her ears. We pat her on the way in and on the way out and sometimes we sit down on the steps with her and cry.

———————

What did I know about Maisie? Not much, just scraps. She had white hair and she was 'five foot five and shrinking'. That's what she told us anyway.

'Then you're five foot four, Maze,' I said.

'A little bit more than that dear, a little more … you're always a bit more than you think you are.'

Maze weighed eight stone five, she told me. Eight of the boulders at the bottom of the garden, eight of those rocks that fall down the hill like Jack and Jill in the stories she read to us; eight of those pebbles I picked up from the beach and put on top of my book to keep it flat. At eight stone my grandmother was both heavy and light. One day, she might just roll away.

———————

When are grandmothers born? Nobody knows that either. What year was Miss Marple born? Before or after Queen Victoria? Sometime *after* Queen Victoria was dead, I think, perhaps before the king of England *abdicated*. 'Abdicated' means he left the throne; got up and walked off and left that shiny polished throne right behind him.

'Flounced out,' Maisie said. 'He flounced right out to that beaming woman with her handbag.'

The king of England flounced right out of his throne room. He ab-di-ca-ted. The king got his sums wrong on the abacus. He pulled too many red balls over when he was counting. Or he began a different sum and no one could make sense of it: not all the kings and queens of England added up together, and one white king with one red wife meant that the one in the middle, in between, wasn't a queen. She wasn't even a lady. Her name begins with W and it sounds like a man's name.

'What was he thinking, rushing off to that woman with her big red lipstick and smile … that woman with her pointy elbows? She has too much powder on her face! It isn't decent! Too much powder and not enough sense! Powder should stay on babies' bottoms!'

Maze spoke as though she had been there, in the crowds outside Buckingham Palace, standing at the front. Sometime in 1936 Edna May was pushing her way through thick arms and legs, she was pressing her small blue beret to her head. Maze was waving her flag and looking hard for a glimpse of that bad lady with the bright red lipstick and the big white forehead.

'She looked like the moon,' my grandmother said. 'The moon wearing a large smile.'

'Always put on your best smile,' Mum said. 'You never know who might be looking. Now wipe off that silly grin and go and wash your hands.'

History is remembered by a series of smiles.

3

THE VILLAGE

She lives in a village, the kind of village where nothing ever happens, exactly like a stagnant pond.

(*Sleeping Murder*)

In the Miss Marple stories everything begins and ends in the village. Whatever happens in the village, Miss Marple knows about it. People tell her things, often without their knowing. Somehow she's always there, just when someone's spilling the beans. Usually she's sitting in the corner somewhere, like my grandmother with her coffee in the morning, *enjoying a nice bit of peace and quiet. Now shoo!*

Most of the time St Mary Mead is lovely and quiet. Every day is like being on holiday. There are no chores, at least not for Miss Marple. In St Mary Mead, Miss Marple wakes up to breakfast served by a girl called Mavis or Edna or Mary, which by the way is my middle name; she walks to the village shop with a wicker basket; she stops at the green-grocer's, the baker's, the butcher's; then she has tea at the Copper Kettle.

This is the kind of life I dreamed of; and when I closed my eyes and dreamed this is where I would be: in St Mary Mead at the Copper Kettle, having tea and cake in the corner.

―――――――――――

Villages are full of secrets. If I want to know something, Greta will tell me what is going on. Greta is the vicar's wife. She loves secrets; but above all, Greta likes to gossip.

When women gossip they usually sit in circles. Gossiping is going round and round in circles until you come back to the same thing. Usually that's someone's husband or wife, but sometimes it's the maid. Gossiping women are witches making spells from other people's names, women making spells and sipping their tea. Now that I think of it, 'Greta' sounds just like a witch, a good witch.

Greta asks Miss Marple to tea because she hopes she can make her *spill the beans*. Then something might actually happen in St Mary Mead. But Greta doesn't realise how much Miss Marple already knows, how much she can tell about Greta just by looking.

Greta Clementine was the sort of girl who relished a piece of scandal. Miss Marple took a quick glance around the room. There was Miss Wetherby jabbering away, talking loudly about the rise in prices at Dentons.

'Two shillings for a jar of marmalade. That isn't *right*, Rosemary, surely? Disgraceful. Simply disgraceful. I think we should all boycott the place.'

Miss Marple looked back at Greta's flushed face. She's married someone far too old for her, and now she's stuck inside this village with nothing to do except listen to idle gossip.

Miss Marple looks carefully at Greta. The poor man couldn't help himself. She's a very pretty little thing, very lively, dresses nicely, nice figure. Still, it was rather selfish of him, because she'll get bored. She's terribly bored already. Look at her fidgeting away. Poor thing, she won't get much from us that isn't commonplace. And she won't get it from her sweet vicar. He's only interested in learning his psalms!

Greta lifted the big brown teapot and turned to Miss Marple eagerly.

'Do you think it's ready, Miss Marple?'

'Oh, I should think so, dear.'

What a sweet old lady, Greta thought. She looks as though she knows everything but she just won't say. Oh, *why* won't she say? Why won't someone tell me something *interesting* about someone at last?

Greta picks up her teacup and sighs. She catches Miss Marple looking at her and smiles.

———————

Let me tell you something about Mummy, because I'd like to spill the beans.

Mummy grew up in a village called Sompting. Sompting is a place in Sussex next to Lancing and Lancing is near Worthing and Worthing is a town by the sea.

Mummy went to school in Worthing. She walked to school with her sister Di. Mummy and Di walked to school holding hands.

Mummy and Di spent all their time together. Their favourite thing to do was to draw maps. They walked around Sompting village and made a map of all the places they knew. They put a cross where the church with the tower was, and an oblong for the school, and a square for the village shop. Mummy said she learned to draw maps from reading the Milly-Molly-Mandy books. They have those in the library. I've read all of them now. The librarian says she can't get me any more because the person who wrote the books has run out of ideas. Or perhaps she's having a baby. Or perhaps she's found a better way to spend her time, gardening. In any case, there aren't any more Milly-Molly-Mandy books so I will have to find something else to read.

Every Milly-Molly-Mandy book begins with a map. If you follow the map you can pretend you are walking around Milly-Molly-Mandy's village. I follow the names of the roads with my finger until I get to the Nice White Cottage with the Thatched Roof where Milly-Molly-Mandy lives; then I go next door to Billy Blunt's house and ask him to come and play.

Billy Blunt lives with Mr Blunt and Mr Blunt owns a shop in the village. Billy gives me sweets from his dad's shop, but I think sometimes he steals them when his dad isn't looking. Billy Blunt's pockets are always stuffed with sweets.

I read the Milly-Molly-Mandy books before I read Agatha

Christie. Those were my very first books, after Peter and Jane, which we had to read at school, so slowly I nearly died. There are no murders in Peter and Jane and there are no murders in Milly-Molly-Mandy's village, but there are lots of cottages with roses round the door. There's Mr Blunt's sweet shop which Mummy says reminds her of the sweet shop in the village where she grew up.

In Milly-Molly-Mandy's village there is a girl called Sue; everyone calls her Sweet Sue. Sweet Sue is Milly-Molly-Mandy's best friend from school. Sweet Sue and Milly-Molly-Mandy spend a lot of time together. They put buttercups under their chins to see which of them likes butter best. '*A little bit of butter and a slice of white bread*,' they sing.

Milly-Molly-Mandy and Sweet Sue make daisy chains; they put them on top of their heads and then they twirl around and around. 'Now you are the May Queen,' says Sue to Milly-Molly-Mandy. 'We shall go dancing upon the green. Put your plimsolls on Milly-Molly-Mandy, you don't want to ruin your nice new white socks.'

Sue and Milly-Molly-Mandy are very happy together. Sue is now Milly-Molly-Mandy's best friend.

Sweet Sue and Milly-Molly-Mandy are always seen around the village together. Mrs Mount at the greengrocer's says they are inseparable. Every day Milly-Molly-Mandy and Sweet Sue walk to school holding hands. Mr Blunt watches them through the sweet-shop window. He knows they will pass every weekday morning at half past eight and that either Sue or Milly-Molly-Mandy will stop and pull up one of their socks just outside his gate. Then he will see a flash of pale rose skin beneath a white cotton hem.

At a quarter past eight every morning, Mr Blunt is ready at the window; he's waiting for the sweet girl with dark brown plaits and her fair-haired friend. Mr Blunt knows too that every afternoon at four o'clock they will come back past his shop. They will step inside and buy either a quarter ounce of sherbet bonbons or a quarter of licorice allsorts. The fair-haired girl prefers the sherbet and the dark-haired likes licorice. He always adds an extra one or two because he wants them to come back.

Mr Blunt closes the shop at six o'clock. He pulls down the strip blinds and looks out across the green. He sees Milly-Molly-Mandy and Sue playing with a hoop and ball. He watches and he watches. Beads of sweat begin to form across his brow. The corners of his mouth twist into a smile.

———————————

People say nothing ever happens in villages. But that isn't true. A lot goes on. Miss Marple knows this. Peculiar things happen in English villages all the time. You only need think of Poor Sue Blunt.

One day over tea at the Copper Kettle Miss Marple tells Greta, the vicar's wife, the story of Poor Sue. Greta tries to remember it so she can tell it to someone else.

'As a child, butter wouldn't melt in her mouth. But she grew up into an odd woman … Poor Sue.'

Miss Marple paused and looked out the window.

'Please do go on, Miss Marple.' Greta looked anxious. She did *so* wish that Miss Marple would stop being so vague and distracted. Miss Marple turned back to Greta. The poor girl was looking worried.

'Something went wrong with Sue. The village people blamed her husband. David Blunt was quiet as a church mouse and very serious. And of course he was far too old for Sue. Three times her age.' Miss Marple paused again. 'Then one day she disappeared.'

'Disappeared?' Greta squeaked, stirring her tea more quickly. 'Someone can't just disappear.'

'Of course they can, dear, if things are managed cleverly.'

'Well she must be somewhere … unless she's dead!'

'Mysterious things happen all the time, dear. You can live alongside people for years and years and not know things about them. Sometimes you are none the wiser for living in such close proximity. Husbands and wives can do the most surprising things …'

Miss Marple suddenly looked serious. 'You can have suspicions, of course. We all have our suspicions.'

'What are your suspicions, Miss Marple?' asked Greta, stirring her tea furiously.

'Sue was tangled up in religion. But it was all too emotional for her. She was a very quiet, modest sort of woman. She wasn't suited to all of that. Sue would have done better as a mother I think.'

'All of what, Miss Marple. All of *what*? Do tell!'

Later, when Greta told Miss Cram over tea at the vicarage, she was disappointed to find that Miss Cram already knew all about it.

'Old enough to be her father. Disgusting,' said Miss Cram. 'It shouldn't have been allowed, a man of over sixty marrying a girl of twenty.' Miss Cram sniffed hard. She opened her bag and pulled out a tissue. She patted her lips.

'And they never had children. I don't think they could. That's the price of unnatural relations if you ask me!'

Greta nursed her hot coffee and looked thoughtful.

'Perhaps. More a case of too much religion and not enough fun. What she needed was more parties instead of prayers. And you know, people say, well …' Greta lowered her head to the table and leaned across towards Miss Cram. 'Well … that they spent all their time, you know …'

'No, I don't know, dear,' said Miss Cram sternly, raising her eyebrow.

Greta leaned in further. 'Summoning spirits … shrieking at God – whatever it is you do when you've gone a bit demented.' She paused and tried to look thoughtful again.

'You've heard that from Jane Marple, I suppose,' said Miss Cram, looking quite put out. 'She oughtn't to be gossiping like that. Doesn't she know it's one of the seven deadly sins?'

4

JANE EYRE AND VERITY

Every story has a backstory. Backstories are stories in disguise. Sleeping Beauty has a backstory, Jane Eyre too, but I should tell you about Sleeping Beauty, because she came first.

Beauty is born to a king and queen who can never have children. For years the royal cot in the palace hallway sits empty. Finally, after ten years, the queen loses hope. She pushes the cot behind the hallway curtains and tells her staff never to touch it again.

Then out of the blue, as if by magic, the queen produces a child, a child so beautiful that anyone who sees him can't help exclaim, 'What a beauty! What a delight! How lucky you are! May God bless you and your child! May he grow fair and tall!'

An old fairy living on the fringes of the palace hears news of the child and she is filled with jealousy. She cannot bear that a child so beautiful and so loved should live. Her heart begins to fill with wicked thoughts.

Every day at noon the child sleeps beneath a rosebush in the garden. One day, the fairy takes a stroll to the rosebush where the child is sleeping. She bends down towards the cot and lifts the white muslin veil that protects him from the sun. Her knobbly fingers are cold and bent and the child, feeling something, stirs. His eyes open and he screams. The fairy pinches the small rosebud mouth between her fingers.

After that, there is only the sound of tweeting.

———————

When people die before their time they turn into ghosts. Ghosts are what the people left behind have to puzzle over. When Miss Marple meets Miss Temple, the school-teacher, she knows she must help her draw out her ghost. Luckily, ghosts can come out of hiding with the mere mention of a name.

'We had been talking,' said Miss Marple, 'about a young girl called Verity.'

'Ah, yes.'

'I did not know her surname. Miss Temple, I think, mentioned her only as Verity.'

'Verity Hunt disappeared years ago,' said the Archdeacon.

'Yes,' said Miss Marple. 'Miss Temple and I were talking about her. Miss Temple told me something I did not know.'

Most ghosts are familiar; you know who they are when you see them. Mum looks like a ghost when she passes down the hallway in her nightie; she's pale all over, grey as congealed porridge. The bottom of her nightie is ripped and torn as if a wild cat has got at it. Sometimes, when the hall light is off, I don't see her coming and I scream. Then Mum gets cross and goes back into her room and slams the door. We don't see her for hours.

Women waft about in their nighties when things are going wrong. Clotilde Bradbury-Scott walks into Miss Marple's room in a purple nightie in the middle of the night because she's afraid. She's had a bad dream about nasty secrets hidden beneath pink polygonum flowers.

'*Polygonum baldschuanicum*. Very quick-growing, I think, isn't it? Very useful really if one wants to hide any tumble-down building or anything ugly of that kind,' says Clotilde.

'Ah, yes, but it's a menace if you want to grow anything else alongside it. Before you can say Jack Robinson your polygonum cover everything.' Clotilde Bradbury-Scott takes a long look at this old woman. Clearly, she knows her plants. Before long she will be volunteering her services in the garden; she must be gone before *that* happens.

People prefer to cover up ghosts, but no matter what you do, ghosts will always go wandering. I met with my first real ghost when I was ten. Her name was Jane Eyre and I found her sitting on the library shelves wearing a tatty brown dress. By then I had run out of Agatha Christie and I was looking for something else. I needed a new friend.

'Adult Fiction,' the librarian said. '*Jane Eyre* is Adult Fiction. Does your mum know you're here?'

'Yes, she knows. She sent me here!'

'Mmm. Well …' The librarian lifted her glasses and peered down her long, thin nose.

'She says I can't keep reading all that murder mystery rubbish. *It's high time I took on the classics!* Agatha Christie isn't literature and no one is going to take me seriously unless I start reading *something more sophisticated.*'

'Mmm. Precocious … I see. Well, she's in Adult Fiction. Over there. Now go quietly. You're really too young to be in there messing about.'

So I crossed the wide, squeaky floor and there, on the other side of that broad wooden stretch I found her in an old brown dress: Jane Eyre, dusty and faded around the edges. Jane Eyre, who is looking for Verity.

———

You won't believe me, but one evening while I was reading something floated down from the glass panels above my head and landed on my page. *Whoosh!* I turned and there she was. I knew it was her immediately. Who else could it be?

I could see her from the corner of my eye, a small pale face staring right at me. She was wearing the same brown dress and a small velvet scarf around her head. Red velvet was blocking my view of the page; red velvet was speaking; red velvet was speaking the words I was reading:

Folds of scarlet drapery shut in my view to the right hand; to the left were clear panes of glass, protecting, but not separating me from the drear November day. At intervals, while turning over the leaves of my book, I studied the aspect of that winter afternoon.

I heard the words enter my brain, and they felt strange. I'd never heard words like this before. Nobody I knew uses words like this. Nobody says drapery when they mean curtains. Drapery is something you hang over something in order to disguise it. Drapery hides things – bodies and knives. Drapery is Jane Eyre behind the red curtains hiding from John Reed (her nasty cousin), who would like to kill her, because John Reed is *not* a good reader. He's jealous of curious Jane, his clever cousin. John Reed has no curiosity. He can't think of anything but his own nasty self! 'No imagination,' Mum says. 'Too caught up in himself. It'll end badly!'

Jane Eyre is a big reader. She knows that when you read, time just passes. I read and read and time passed, but when I looked up from my book, the strange little person was still there. I wondered where she'd come from. Her face said nothing at all. Her body was thin and her face pale and her hair fell over her face.

'Slides,' said Mum. 'What she needs is some nice tortoiseshell slides. Clip it back, for goodness' sake, Maze. She looks like a wild thing running about with all that hair blowing about. For goodness' sake, get it off her face!'

I hated my slides. They pulled my hair so tight I got a headache. But I couldn't see slides anywhere on Jane Eyre's forehead, only tiny, furrowed lines. Jane Eyre was too focused on reading to think about her hair.

'You're a very serious person, Jane Eyre,' I said out loud.

'Maze says it's good to keep a sense of fun. *You mustn't be too serious before your time.* I don't know how old you are, but you can't be much older than me, and I'm eleven at the end of the summer as a matter of fact. And Maze says *you can't afford to be too serious too soon.* If you're too serious then no one will want you around. For one thing, you won't get invited to any parties and no one will want to dance with you at the school fête and you'll never ever be chosen as the May Queen or get a part in the school play. You're not tall enough for that. I wasn't chosen because I'm not as tall as Melissa Marshall and I'm not as pretty as Rachel Green, but I've got a good speaking voice, so Miss Bellamy chose me as the school narrator, and I don't mind that. What about you, Jane Eyre, what will *you* be?'

But the little person with the pale face just blinked and turned back to her book.

———————

She stayed for hours. I can't tell how many. Sometimes I looked up and I saw her mouth moving. I heard her quiet whispers. But she ignored me. She didn't want to talk. She just kept on reading. (I think I hurt her feelings about the play, but truthfully, she would *never* get a part.) Jane Eyre, I decided, was a serious sort of person, and serious people never quite relax.

'Clever people can be very tiresome,' Maze says. 'Cousin Norman was an *intellectual* and he was *very taxing. They just can't switch off. Too much going on upstairs … Norman could never relax.*'

But after a while I did. I relaxed right into my book and soon I forgot she was there. Hours passed. Before long it was dark and Maze was coming to bed.

And that is when things began to change. That night there were clear panes of glass running between everyone else and me and I was suddenly quite separate, stuck on a solitary rock, far out at sea.

———

By the time I'd finished reading *Jane Eyre* I knew that you can find missing people inside books. Jane Eyre, who reads a lot of books, calls these *natural sympathies*. Sympathies are relatives you never knew you had, the ones you always wanted. Sympathies are family ghosts and fairies, and sympathies keep you up at night.

I decided that my sympathies were Jane Eyre and Miss Marple, and once upon a time, a long time before I was born, they had been walking together through an English village looking for Verity.

'Verity! Verity! Verity!'

But Verity disappeared years ago! Because someone loved her too much.

You can kill people you love, you know. In mysteries, this happens all the time. Miss Marple knows this, and Jane Eyre too, because like Miss Marple, Jane Eyre sees and hears everything; and like Miss Marple, she is genteel.

'She looks like a lady,' says Bessie Lee when she finds Jane all grown up. Bessie, who used to help her wash and dress, but not kindly; Bessie, who was too afraid of Aunt Reed to be kind.

'Just like a lady now, Miss Jane, very proper. Look at you!'

Bessie means that Jane Eyre is small and quiet and demure, so people don't see her coming round the corner, or across the village green with a basket in her hand. They don't see her coming in through the back door and climbing up the stairs. Jane Eyre is quiet as a mouse. But she wanders everywhere, swifter than the moon's sphere. And what she sees, she doesn't tell a soul.

———————

'Over hill, over dale, Thorough bush, thorough brier, Over park, over pale, thorough flood, thorough fire, I do wander everywhere, Swifter than the moon's sphere, And I serve the fairy queen, To dew her orbs upon the green.'

That's Mum's favourite part of Shakespeare; she says it out loud sometimes. When I first heard those lines I thought she was speaking about Jane Eyre and Mr Rochester, the master of Thornfield Hall; Mr Rochester, the man Jane loves and leaves in the lurch.

But Mum said it was Shakespeare. 'Only Shakespeare can write lines like that.'

Mum loves her Shakespeare. I think she likes Jane Eyre too, but she knows some bits of Shakespeare off by heart. She had to learn them at school. If she got them wrong the teacher, who was very strict, rapped her on the knuckles with a ruler. Mum says school *back then* wasn't exactly like Lowood School where Jane is sent by horrid Aunt Reed, but *something not far off.*

Now I think of it, I'm not sure Mum would like Jane Eyre. She has a nose for secrets. Jane Eyre is curious; she listens in. Mum would say she's a nosey parker, but Jane Eyre knows that plenty of things go on behind closed doors if you listen carefully. Like Mr Rochester's dog, Pilot, she can sniff out the sinister and strange. Beware all those who house Jane Eyre!

Mrs Fairfax stayed behind a moment to fasten the trapdoor. I, by dint of groping, found the outlet from the attic, and proceeded to descend the narrow garret staircase. I lingered in the long passage to which this led, separating the front and back rooms of the third story – narrow, low, and dim, with only one little window at the far end, and looking, with its two rows of small black doors all shut, like a corridor in some Bluebeard's castle.

'Mrs Fairfax!' I called out – for now I heard her descending the great stairs. 'Did you hear that loud laugh? Who is it?'

(*Jane Eyre*)

When you read a book like *Jane Eyre*, you start to see things, small fragments of this and that that shoot across your eyes like stars. Tiny pictures appear in between the pages as you turn them. You begin to see and hear things: a woman's smile, a woman's laugh, a woman with her hands held high, a woman speaking gobbledygook. And then suddenly, without warning, you are in Lancing on Sea a long time ago and you don't know how you got there. Some strange spirit has carried you away. *Jane Eyre! Jane Eyre! Whither wander you?*

5

DI

I remember Di. She was the woman who arrived one night when I was five. Di was the woman who came from behind the dark curtains and sat in spirals of smoke. Di was the woman with a baby who cried in the night. Di was the woman with the long, snaky smile. Di was the woman who spoke gobbledygook. Di was the woman in my dreams.

One day, Mum took me upstairs to say hello to Di, the woman with black bullet eyes.

'She's your aunt, darling, your Aunt Diane. She's come to live with us. She's had a baby. We're going to look after her. Now say hello nicely.'

What was an aunt, I wondered. I had never heard of *an aunt* before. What did aunts come from?

'From Lancing on Sea,' Mum said. 'From Lancing on Sea.'

A few days later, my brother Peter and I found a body in the front room. We came home from school and there was a man lying on the floor. He was thin with a black moustache and black hair and his mouth hung wide open. My brother opened the door and tripped over him.

'He's dead! He's dead! Peter, Peter, it's a dead body! We've found a dead body! Call the police!'

The dead man looked like a large black ant. I felt sorry for him. We could easily squash him and no one would ever know. Here was a poor dead ant, stuck to our hard floor. A giant spider or fly must have come from behind the curtains and strangled him.

Mummy came in and told us off for making such a fuss. The man on the floor was *a friend of Aunt Di*. Think of him as your uncle, she said. Uncle David. Uncle David is sleeping now, so *shhhhh! Now close the door quietly behind you! There's a baby upstairs!*

———

When you start a murder investigation you have to have clear plans of the place where the murder happened. Detectives call this the 'crime scene'. If the crime scene is in a house they draw up careful room plans. Everything that might have happened has to be kept inside closed lines. Nothing must straggle over the edges. Detectives don't like mess.

But a detective would have found our house difficult to plan. In fact, Inspector Craddock would have hated our house. (Miss Marple thinks Inspector Craddock is hopeless, but she's too polite to say so.) Still, the inspector has a point: you can't be a good detective among muddle and mess.

'Where is my nice pair of scissors?' Mum yelled down the hallway. 'Which of you little swines has got my sewing scissors? Can't I leave anything out without you getting your filthy hands on it!'

Fortunately, Miss Marple has an excellent memory so she doesn't need to draw up plans. She can draw her own lines around things. Miss Marple can remember what lamp was on when the gun went off. She can recall which door was open and which was closed. She can remember exactly who was there and who wasn't, precisely how the curtains sat on the carpet, who sneezed just before the light went out.

———————

Everything I know comes from reading. Everything I've found out comes because of Miss Marple and then Jane Eyre.

After I found Jane Eyre nothing was the same again. She was always there, always looking and hearing the things no one else dared. Let me show you what I mean.

One night, in her small room at Thornfield Hall, Jane Eyre hears a strange gurgling sound coming from the room above her. She stirs and opens her eyes, but she can't see anything in front of her except smoke! Smoke is filling the hallway outside her room, smoke is pushing its way beneath her door, smoke is filling up her lungs.

Jane leaps out of bed and races down the hall; she flies towards Mr Rochester's room and shouts through the door. 'Master, Master, wake up! Wake up! Your room is on fire!'

Lucky for Mr Rochester, Jane is a quick thinker. Quick as a flash, says Maze, fast on her feet, that one. Doesn't miss a trick. And Jane is practical, too. She drags Mr Rochester out of bed and takes him to safety, to the hallway (the *gallery*, the Victorians call it, where pictures of dead ancestors hang) outside her room. Mr Rochester knows that, without Jane, he would be dead.

'Dead as a dormouse,' Maze says about the brown furry thing the cat has brought in. Mr Rochester might not be dead as a dormouse exactly, but he'd be dead as *something* without Jane. That night he takes her into his confidence forever; that night Jane becomes his fairy-friend.

The next morning Jane starts asking some serious questions on behalf of her new friend.

'I am certain I heard a laugh, and a strange one,' she announces to Mr Rochester's servant Grace Poole the following morning. 'It can't have been Pilot, because Pilot can't laugh.' Pilot is a dog.

Grace lifts her needle, takes a new ball of thread, waxes it, pokes the end through and carries on sewing. Her face doesn't flinch, not even a bit. Jane is furious. Last night Mr Rochester told her that the strange laugh was Grace Poole. Grace Poole must have tried to burn Mr Rochester in bed. Jane is sure of it! She saw his bed: the curtains around it were burnt to a cinder. Mr Rochester is lucky to be alive! Grace Poole is a monster! She should be locked up!

'I am certain I heard a laugh.'

'Have you told Master that you heard a laugh?' asks Grace

quietly. 'You did not think of opening your door and looking out into the gallery?'

'On the contrary,' says Jane Eyre, who is beginning to get huffy. 'I bolted my door!'

'And you are not in the habit of bolting your door every night?'

'I have often omitted to fasten my door. I was not aware any danger or annoyance was to be dreaded at Thornfield Hall?'

'I always think it is best to err on the safe side; a door is soon fastened, and it is as well to have a drawn bolt between one and any mischief that may be about. A deal of people, Miss, are for trusting all to Providence.'

Jane looks at the placid face of the woman in front of her. A Quaker woman couldn't produce more serenity than this woman with her needle. Why has she not been taken into police custody for her criminal behaviour? Mr Rochester was nearly burned alive in his bed last night by this fiend with her uncanny laugh!

Jane pauses for a moment. Grace is hiding something. It was a woman's laugh she heard, she is certain, the laugh of an angry witch. A woman burying bones at nightfall.

6

BEHIND CLOSED DOORS

Some houses have no chance in hell of becoming homes. Thornfield Hall is one of these. It is home neither to Jane Eyre nor Mr Rochester; both come and go from it like fairies.

'In what order you keep these rooms, Mrs. Fairfax!' says Jane Eyre to the housekeeper soon after she arrives.

'Why Miss Eyre, though Mr. Rochester's visits here are rare, they are always sudden and unexpected; and as I observed that it put him out to find everything swathed up, and to have a bustle of arrangement on his arrival, I thought it best to keep the rooms in readiness.'

In our house, rooms were never ready. We didn't have a Mrs Fairfax to dust and pull back the curtains, to hoover up the filth or scrub down the surfaces. We didn't have a Mrs Fairfax to let in the light.

Mr Robinson was the only person we could ever imagine visiting. Mr Robinson who lived on the third floor, right at the top, with his wife, Mrs Robinson, who we never saw. Mr Robinson was the only person who would poke his head through our door if we left it open; Mr Robinson suddenly standing in our front room with boxes of farm eggs in his arms; Mr Robinson suddenly at the window with his long scraggy dark hair and cracked-tooth smile.

———————

But anyone can barge into your dreams.

One night, Jane sees a woman in her room, a woman with long dark hair. Birds circle around her head; wings cover her lips and eyes, her nose and mouth, her face.

Suddenly Jane sees a garish red face and startling black eyes bearing down on her. A dark cavern opens up, and at the back of the cavern is a red serpent lifting its head and hissing. The woman begins to scream. She drops to the floor and begins to writhe. She writhes and she writhes and then she opens her mouth wide.

Jet-black rocks tumble from her mouth. Black rocks spill across the room and hit Jane on the face. Before long there is nothing but the cold dark and black sea, the sound of waves against her ear.

———————

Mr Robinson had murdered Mrs Robinson. We knew this because we never ever saw her. Not once, not ever, not after all these years.

Maisie said she had seen her, just the once, early one morning when she was coming in with the milk. But we never had. We'd *never* seen Mrs Robinson and we were *sure* that Mr Robinson had killed Mrs Robinson. Mr Robinson was a big fat liar!

Mr Robinson, we decided, needed watching. So we climbed to the top of the house to listen for the sound of his breathing. We wanted to see if we could hear anyone breathing behind that dark door.

We pressed our ears to the door. But the door was thick. We strained and strained to hear something. My brother stuck a piece of string through the keyhole and wiggled it. He tugged and tugged at the key to try to make it fall. Then he stuck his fingers under the bottom of the door until he felt the silver key. The key was hard and cold. He squeezed and squeezed his fingers into the narrow crack until they were red and torn. Then he shone his torch on his fingers, and that's when we saw the blood. Blood all over his fingers. We screamed and ran downstairs and Mum came out and said, *Shhhhh! For Pete's sake, I'm trying to sleep!*

But after a while we went back up. We went back again and again. We peered through the keyhole until our eyes hurt because we were absolutely sure of this: Mrs Robinson had been lying on the kitchen floor with blood caked to her face for years. Mr Robinson was a big fat liar!

I have at several times in my life recognized that there was evil in the neighbourhood, the surroundings, that the environment of someone who was evil was near me, connected with what was happening.

Miss Marple (*Nemesis*)

Where were you when it all happened, that's what you need to know. Where were *you*, and where was *everyone else*? If Miss Marple wanted to find out what had happened she would start by asking some questions, some very particular questions.

'What happened, dear? Can you remember where you were when it happened? Who were you standing next to? What were you wearing? Were you holding anything in your hands? What happened the moment, the very moment, when the man with the dazzling light and the gun said "Stick 'em up"?'

And I would say: 'I remember the back door standing open and Mummy with a pale face and her hair lit up like a lamp. Mummy's face wasn't moving; she looked like a ghost. Mummy was a ghost come back from the dead and the man next to her was saying something in a language I couldn't understand. He had a red face and no hair and Mummy wasn't moving at all. Mummy was as still as a statue. The man with the red face was the only one talking, and all the time the light kept shining through Mummy's hair, shining and shining and shining. And that is all I could look at, Mummy's hair, which was as neat as a haystack.'

The only word I remember from that day is 'hospital'. Mummy and the man with no hair said they were going to the hospital. And I thought, hospitals are for sick people or for children who have bashed their heads.

That day Mummy went into her bedroom and shut the door. She went into her room and closed the curtains. She got into bed with her clothes on. Mummy stayed in bed for years, until the day the lady in brown came round with her notepad and began to ask questions.

7

POOR SUE

They were whispering together for half-an-hour before
they fell asleep. I caught scraps of their conversation, from
which I was able only too distinctly to infer the main
subject discussed.

(Jane Eyre)

If you listen carefully, you can work out things that adults
don't tell you. You can hear small scraps, words floating
through windows on a hazy summer day. If you sit outside the
kitchen window downstairs you can hear Mum and Maze
whispering. You can hear bits and pieces of Poor Sue coming
your way on the breeze.

Poor Sue was married to a man. His name was David, like
my brother. Sue and David were married for a while and then
something interrupted it, the being married I mean. I strain my
ears but I can't tell you any more than that because the wind
keeps scooping up the words. The words never get any further
than the washing line before the line strangles the words.

Mum speaks Greek but she doesn't like me listening because she says it's *personal* and *private*. Greek is a special gift from God. But I don't see how that can be in our house. Nothing is private here.

Private is for someone with a big house with a wooden gate and crunchy gravel stones. *Private* is for the people who live on Maltravers Drive. *Private* is for the girls who go to Rose Mead School in the middle of town. *Private* is a place with pretty flintstone walls around it to keep out the tramps and alcoholics. We could never ever live anywhere *private*.

Still, I know there are private things going on all around me, but I don't know what they are. They aren't the things people usually mean when they say something is private. 'Private' in my house means secrets. 'Private' means Poor Sue.

Of all the ghosts, Sue is the one who has survived. After she went missing, people still mentioned her name. Sue's name never went away, not even after all these years.

'Gone off the rails,' said my aunt wearily. 'She has only herself to blame for the way she went … Sue was a poor little thing … *No real guidance*, that was her trouble … *Married the first man she met. She had nobody to show her a way through.*'

Through what, I wondered? Back through the white door upstairs, back to that front room in 1969, the one I see in my dream.

And the dream is always the same.

It is 1969 and a striking, dark-haired woman sits in the front room of a terraced house marrying herself off to Jesus. Her altarpiece is a brocade-covered television. Her nave is an orange and brown carpet. Across her face a white mantilla veil rises and falls. White lace touches the edge of her tongue. She kisses it softly. She is a young bride marrying her lover. Tonight she will dance with her Lord. Tonight her kingdom will come.

'Lift your eyes unto the Lord, unto the Lord!' And the cross-legged people look up towards the ceiling; the cross-legged people lift their hands in prayer.

'Christ is near, oh Christ is near, Christ, He is near. Oh Christ we hear you, oh Christ you are near. Draw near!'

Her head rocks and her eyes close into tight black buds. Her mouth falls open. What comes out is neither English nor human. It is the sound of women in long-forgotten temples, women with their tongues cut out. It is the sound of madness, of the moon caught between the trees, howling.

The lights go out. A woman screams. Someone tears a nail.

The dark-haired woman begins to rise and fall. Her tongue flicks in and out; her head falls backwards.

Suddenly, hot rocks fly across the room. A window smashes.

'Gooolagoooolagoooolagah. Gooolagooooolagooooolaha.' Glass begins to fly.

My aunt has caught the sound of God in the back of her throat and is wailing with all her might.

But I had started to tell you about Poor Sue. Sue wasn't exactly real any more because she had disappeared, but once upon a time Sue really was there. She was there in the garden, by the back door; there in the blue and white kitchen drinking tea with the people wearing coloured clothes; the people who sang songs about Zion and Babylon; the people who came in and out through the back door with long hair; the people who lifted their faces up to the Lord. Sue was there too, lifting her hands to the Lord, and it is Sue who reminds me of Jane Eyre, or Jane Eyre who reminds me of Sue, who Charlotte Brontë says is a small brown bird.

Years later, someone told me that Sue had been an orphan too, like Jane. I think it was Someone's Mother. Sue had no mother, she said, no people of her own, so the people of Babylon, the people I see in my dreams, scooped her up and took her to a tower where they gave her a room overlooking the sea.

Where the Northern Ocean, in vast whirls,
Boils round the naked, melancholy isles
Of farthest Thule; and the Atlantic surge
Pours in among the stormy Hebrides.

(*Jane Eyre*)

The first thing I remember about Sue is that she was small and plain. If you say someone is small and plain it probably means you're not very fond of them. If you say, instead, that someone is slight and shy then you are probably trying to redeem them. Maze says you should always focus on *the redeeming features*. I wouldn't say that Sue was small and plain, but someone else might, someone who didn't like her very much.

Sue wore brown, and brown is hard to hold on to. Brown blurs in with everything else: with the horse chestnut at the bottom of our garden; with the conkers on the ground we gathered up and baked in the oven; with the grass that very hot summer when the water ran out; with the shade of my brother's skin; with the colour of the picnic blanket my grandmother put down to protect us from the heat; with the back of my grandmother's hand after she'd been peeling potatoes and digging up the beans. Brown is the colour of small creatures that lie close to the ground. Brown is the colour of worms and small birds.

To say that Sue was small and brown is to say nothing at all. It is to say that she resembled a sparrow, and sparrows are very common.

'In England, sparrows are the most common form of bird,' says Maze, who knows everything about birds and beans. Jane Eyre is a sparrow. She is Jane who takes to the air, Jane with no perch, Jane with no family. But once upon a time, Jane Eyre did have family. Jane's uncle was a nice man called Mr Reed, but unfortunately for Jane he is dead. Only his awful wife remains. Mrs Reed has adopted Jane, but Mrs Reed doesn't really want her. Jane knows that her aunt hates her and her aunt knows that she knows this, and so it goes on: the hating and the concealing and then the seeing.

'What would Uncle Reed say to you if he were alive?' Jane screams at her aunt one morning. But once she's begun, Jane can't stop herself. Mrs Reed is furious and lashes out; she boxes Jane's ears. She can't believe her insolence!

They are not fit to associate with me!' screams Jane Eyre.

Mrs Reed was rather a stout woman; but on hearing this strange and audacious declaration, she ran nimbly up the stairs, swept me like a whirlwind into the nursery, and crushing me on the edge of my crib, dared me in an emphatic voice to rise from that place, or utter one syllable during the remainder of the day … she boxed both my ears, and then left me without a word.

I'm not quite sure what 'boxing ears' means, but I think it means slapping someone very hard around the side of the head so that they are knocked unconscious. The white stars soon arrive. An ambulance has to be called.

Mrs Reed locks Jane in the Red Room and leaves her there for days. Her only wish now is to get her out of her sight; and so Jane is sent to Lowood School, where she is starved and beaten and frozen almost to death.

8

ROCKS FROM THE SKY

One day, not so long ago, someone called an ambulance to our house. That was the day God sent a plague of rocks down from the sky.

The day my brother Peter knocked his head hard on the paraffin heater; the heater that stands in the corner with sharp metal edges Mum is always telling us to stay away from. That day Peter banged his head and saw the stars. A few weeks later another ambulance came and carried Poor Sue away. We only saw her toes poking out from the back of the van. I caught a glimpse of a small pink hand and a tiny red beak, and I thought that Sue was done for. The black rocks had knocked her unconscious; the black rocks had boxed her ears. Sue had been crushed by the black rocks tumbling from the sky.

But I am mixing Poor Sue and Peter together. Was it Peter and then Sue, or Sue then Peter? There were two ambulances. When David went away we never heard the ambulance. We didn't see the men in white rushing out. We never saw his body, only Mummy standing by the kitchen door looking like a ghost.

But once upon a time Sue was there and she was lying stretched out in an ambulance with her little toe poking through the gap in the door. Then there was my brother Peter; there was Peter with his broken head and Mummy speaking her Greek and me staring out the kitchen window waiting for the ambulance to come. I look up at the sky and I see dark clouds; I see Mrs Sturgess at the window next door looking down at me. I look up at Mrs Sturgess and I poke out my tongue. Then I feel bad.

So I turn back towards the kitchen table and there is Mummy with her mouth wide open and black rocks falling out.

'Cummmmingleeeenghaawghulalghulaa, ghulala, ghulala, ghulala, cumingleeeehawghulaghulaghula, cummingleeeeing-hawwghulaghulaghula.'

Mummy is humming like a bee. Her mouth is writhing like a snake. I am six or seven and Mummy's mouth is filling up with rocks and the rocks are tumbling onto the floor. I can hear the sharp bang.

'Mummy, Mummy, are you hurt? Shut your mouth, Mummy, shut your mouth. Mummy, please shut your mouth.'

'Ghuuulllllllllllaaaparrrwarrrrrrbarralllungungungung.'

'Mummy, Mummy, is he dead? Is he dead? Is Peter dead? Mummy, please bring him back. Bring him back, Mummy, please, please bring him back.'

It was Mrs Sturgess next door who heard the wailing through the walls and made the call. When the ambulance men came in through the back door Mummy was holding Peter tightly, rocking him back and forth and my brother was as still and quiet as a perfectly behaved baby Jesus.

'Mummy, is Peter coming back to life now? Mummy, has God saved him? Mummy, can he breathe now? *Can he breathe?*'

'Yes, darling. Peter has come back to us. We must thank God for his special words. We must remember this special occasion. AH-MEN.' And then Mummy's head fell forward and the dark rocks came spilling out.

———————

One morning, a few months after the boxing of her ears, Jane Eyre is hiding away in the nursery, making shapes from the frost on the window. She sees a small robin, a hungry little robin *that came and chirruped on the twigs of the leafless cherry-tree nailed against the wall near the casement.* Suddenly Bessie the maid bursts into the room and demands that Jane get herself ready to come downstairs. *She is wanted by Aunt Reed, this minute!*

So Jane is scooped up by Bessie and taken down to the front parlour, where she meets a *black pillar* of a man standing with his legs wide apart. His name is Mr Brocklehurst and he is a servant of God.

'Well Jane Eyre, and are you a good child?' asks Mr Brocklehurst.

But before Jane can answer, Aunt Reed butts in: '*Mr. Brocklehurst, I believe … that this little girl has not quite the character and disposition I could wish. We must send her away, I want this child out of my sight! Out of my sight! Far away!'*

9

DAVID COPPERFIELD

By the time I was ten I had read all of Agatha Christie and I practically knew *Jane Eyre* off by heart. I was ready for something new. 'Proper Literature!' Mum said. 'Now go and find some Dickens! None of this murder mystery nonsense!'

So I went to the library with a list of names. *Oliver Twist … Barnaby Rudge … David Copperfield.* I thought I'd try a book about a David. This was difficult, because the lady at the desk was watching me like a hawk.

'Young lady, can I help you?'

'I'm looking for a book by Charles Dickens,' I said.

'Dickens! What does a child like you want with Dickens? You can't be more than nine.'

'Actually, I'm ten and a bit. I'm an August birthday.'

'Don't be so silly,' said the brown jumper and hair. 'You aren't ready for Dickens.'

'Mum says I am!'

'Does she now? Humph.'

'Well, I can't keep reading *Jane Eyre*, can I? Mum says I need to start something new.'

The brown glasses lifted and a pair of dark narrow eyes and wispy eyebrows flew towards me. Worms, bookworms, I thought. Urgh!

'Well, I don't mind you going to have a quick browse. But be sure that you don't take any more than two books at a time. We have limited copies and I don't want our *adult* readers left …' The eyebrows were wriggling fast across the floor. Soon they would be on top of my toes and I would have to run. '… *wanting.*'

Wanting what, I wondered as I skittered into the large reading room. Wanting *what* exactly?

Charles Dickens was easy to find. He had rows and rows of old bound books with titles that were hard to read because they were written in gold lettering and the lettering had nearly come off. *D—d Copp—f-eld*. I picked up the book and opened the pages. The paper was so thin I thought it would tear. My hands were hot and sticky and stuck to the small print. I let go and the pages fell open. I peered at the words, which were small and narrow and pressed tight together. I started to read.

There comes out of the cloud, our house – not new to me, but quite familiar, in its earliest remembrance. On the ground-floor is Peggotty's kitchen, opening into a back yard … Here is a long passage – what an enormous perspective I make of it! – leading from Peggotty's kitchen to the front door.

———

What comes first when you begin to remember – the person or the place, or is it their face? What do you see first when you close your eyes and press upon their lids? When do those purple circles start to come, along with the white dancing stars? If you want to remember, you have to travel back through those dark purple pools, back to the stars.

Lie under the trees in the back garden and press your fingers tight over your eyes. Start dreaming back past the dark spaces, past the blur and the whirr of other people's voices and faces, back to the child lying beneath the tree in the summer sun, back to the green and the blue and the shapes you know how to draw because they are easy: dark-brown tree trunk, blue sky, green prickly grass, legs in shorts, feet in sandals, a bucket hanging from the tree that someone has thrown up there – your brother. His shout. Then your mother's face looming over the top of you and around her white stars, your mother shooting white stars from the top of her head and the clouds scudding quickly away.

'Young lady, I think it's about time you chose a book, don't you?' *Peggotty?!* I turned around. The brown lady is standing right behind me; her glasses have slipped down her nose and her face looks very hot.

'We're closing in fifteen minutes and I need to sort the shelves. So come along, young lady. Off you go. Hop, skip and jump!'

By the time I began reading *David Copperfield* I had become a full-blown detective, and I knew that the job of a detective is to explain things. Miss Marple always does this, right at the end of the story. She does it with everyone sitting around – with Dolly Bantry, Greta, the vicar, Inspector Flack (who always looks huffy), the Bradbury-Scott sisters, and whichever doctor has been called out to examine the body.

So let me explain a few things. *David Copperfield* is filled with people who aren't family but behave as though they are. First of all there is Peggotty. Peggotty is a mix of my grandmother and Mary the maid from *The Murder at the Vicarage*, but with less banging about. This is Peggotty:

> The first objects that assume a distinct presence before me, as I look far back into the blank of my infancy, are my mother with her pretty hair and youthful shape, and Peggotty with no shape at all, and eyes so dark that they seemed to darken their whole neighbourhood in her face, and cheeks and arms so hard and red that I wondered the birds didn't peck her in preference to apples ...

> (*David Copperfield*)

Peggotty is David's favourite thing. If she really *were* a thing she'd be a pillow, an old, raggedy pillow. Peggotty is the person who holds David's hand when he's falling asleep; Peggotty is the voice above his cot; Peggotty is the hand stroking his hair.

Peggotty is the sudden explosion of laughter when he takes his first step and lands face-down in the vegetable patch. Peggotty is the crease on the side of her cheek. Peggotty can only be seen in small edges and outlines: the dip of her waist, the tightness of the string around her apron, the prick of her lip as she opens her mouth to say 'Coo-chi-coo,' the dent in her forehead when she frowns.

I can remember Peggotty by the smell of the kitchen, by the whiff of the cheese on toast she pulls from the grill when we come back from school, far too early to be called dinner and far too late to be lunch. 'After-school food', we say, food after school, food before bedtime, food before it gets dark, because we don't ever really have a proper dinner. We just eat lots of cheese on toast and sardines on toast and scrambled egg on toast and pilchard sandwiches and boiled eggs because this is all protein and protein makes you grow as tall as Jack and the Beanstalk.

I remember Peggotty by what she did when: Peggotty who does all the chores, Peggotty with her hands deep in the kitchen sink, Peggotty with soap on her hands and in her hair, Peggotty who we make fun of because she counts the slices of cheese before she lays them out on the bread as though they were about to go missing.

'Thieving hands, your naughty thieving hands.'

Peggotty who is never seen without an apron around her waist. Peggotty who stoops over slightly because she has been carrying so much shopping for years. Peggotty who spends a lot of time carrying things up and down stairs. Peggotty who complains about her creaking knees and at night asks us to fetch her slippers.

———————

When David's mother is tired, Peggotty puts out the washing. She waits for a fine day and then carries out the wicker basket with the peg bag tied to her waist. She stands outside pouring herself forwards and backwards like a milk jug over a cup of tea. I watch her tip and turn and swivel as she moves around the line, turning the clothes to face the wind, whispering her laundry prayers.

'This way round, not that. Hang from the bottom, not the top. Keep the crease nice and straight. Don't mix up the colours, keep the socks together. Hang the pullover from the middle. Don't let things hang too close to the ground. Turn the line every hour or so. Bring the washing in as soon as you feel it's dry.'

It is a fine summer's day and Peggotty is pegging out the washing. The washing blows across her face. Then the wind picks up. The washing flaps and flaps, and covers her mouth and her eyes. For a moment, things go blank. She can no longer see the little boy sleeping beneath the roses. Her face begins to furrow and she frowns. All this damn washing in the way! I can't see the child. Where is the boy?

Peggotty drags the damp washing away from her hands, from around her neck, from across her mouth. She screams. The grassy patch beneath the roses is dry and bare as a baby's bottom.

10

PEGGOTTY

The days when my mother and I and Peggotty were
all in all to one another, and there was no one to come
between us, rose up before me so sorrowfully on
the road.

(David Copperfield)

Let me explain a few more things. First of all, Peggotty lives
with David Copperfield's mother (who is called Clara). They
live like husband and wife because David's dad is dead. Mr
Copperfield died six months before David was born, which
was very inconvenient for everyone concerned.

'Selfish,' Mum says. 'Without a thought for anyone else …
what timing!' So now Peggotty and David's mum share the
chores; they share David.

David and David's mum and Peggotty all live together in
the house surrounded by dark elms. They are three and only
one can ever divide three, because three is a prime number. So
they can only ever be three or one, one or three, without any
remainders. This is how it was once in my house too.

Sometime soon after I was born Maisie came to live with Mum. She came to help with the chores. Mum couldn't manage all the nappies; she couldn't face the washing up. Mum wasn't coping, Maisie said. She meant Mum wasn't *copying* very well what other people do when they have children. Mum wasn't making the beds. She wasn't taking out the nappies. She wasn't feeding us beans on toast. She wasn't getting out to the shops. So Maisie came and she stayed forever and this was our first house.

This was the house with the back door that never closed, the house that led into a garden with a path we turned into the river, the River Arun rushing out to meet the sea. And on that river we held boat races and imagined we were the speedboats on the harbour front racing through white spray towards the seagulls sitting on the end of the pier. And under the apple tree, which hadn't yet been cut down, we threw our buckets up to see who could reach the highest branch. And we tied our boats to the tree trunk and sat and pretended to eat fish and chips off the front and laughed at the speedboats going by much slower than we were and waved and waved and waved. And the apple blossom fell on top of our noses and in our eyes and we saw the white stars come out again and we lay down beneath the tree and fell asleep until Maisie came out with her clippers and told us that the green beans needed tying up and that our feet were in the way.

And now I see outside of our house, with the latticed bedroom windows standing open to let in the sweet-smelling air, and the ragged old rooks' nests still dangling in the elm-trees at the bottom of the front garden. Now I am in the garden at the back, beyond the yard where the empty pigeon-house and dog-kennel are – a very preserve of butterflies, as I remember it, with a high fence, and a gate, and a padlock; where the fruit clusters on the trees, riper and richer than fruit has ever been since, in any other garden.

(*David Copperfield*)

———————

In the first house, my grandmother and I shared a dark bedroom with pink shells. Some days she would pick up her shells and push them to my ear.

'Listen to the sea. If you talk to the sea, it will talk back. Listen to the sea, and it will take you somewhere nice.'

I picked up the shell with its curly horns and put it to my ear. I thought I heard the faint sound of the sea, and behind that, the sound of my grandmother laughing. I push the shell harder to my ear. I can hear the lapping of the waves, and behind that, other things: voices, shrieks, a young woman giggling, a young woman kicking her legs through the air and flying; a young woman with spots of rouge on her cheeks smiling up at a man called Cyril.

'Cyril, Cyril, you'll make me fall!' Her voice is high and squeaky. My grandmother is a pink-faced mouse tripping over her tail. The man in front of her is making her dizzy. She wishes he wouldn't.

My grandmother misses a step and giggles. Edna May Turner is paying too much attention to the look of Cyril Cooper and his curly moustache, Cyril who keeps treading on her toes, Cyril who pulls her closer towards him, Cyril who lowers his face towards her and whispers, Cyril who keeps making her blush.

'Cyril, stop it! I can't concentrate.'

It is Saturday night and my grandmother is dancing the Charleston with two left feet and a long tail.

———————

Some Saturdays when she wasn't dancing, my grandmother went to the beach. Sometime in the 1930s, my grandmother Edna May sat on Shoreham beach holding her hat tight to her head. The wind blew up her stockings and under her skirt and she fussed and fretted and giggled at the bumps of air running up and down her legs.

'Look, Gladys, look! There's a mouse up my skirt. Get it out, Gladys, get it out!'

Her sisters Gladys and Peg poked and petted her and told her to stop all her squawking.

'What would Cyril think if he were here? You're behaving like a perfect ninny. Stop your squealing, Maze.'

I've seen a photograph of Maisie on the beach. She keeps it in her purse. In the photograph she has white gloves on. At least, they look white in the photograph. I stare at the gloves.

I want to take them off and touch her hands. I want to feel the wet soft soap bubbles on her fingers. I want those bubbles to last forever, those little rings on the ends of her fingers that feel for the rough parts, that rub in the soap.

> I have an impression on my mind which I cannot
> distinguish from actual remembrance, of the touch of
> Peggotty's forefinger as she used to hold it out to me, and
> of its being roughened by needlework, like a pocket
> nutmeg-grater.

(*David Copperfield*)

II

BETSEY TROTWOOD

And then, out of the blue, a long-lost relative comes to visit, a family remainder, somebody everyone had completely forgotten about. One day, a strange woman in a bulging hat suddenly appears at David Copperfield's house.

That afternoon, David's mother (whose name is Clara) looks out the window and sees a '*formidable personage*' coming down the garden path. As a matter of fact, by the time we hear about the Formidable Personage she is already peering in through the window, which, when you're wearing a large hat, is as good as inviting yourself in. The Formidable Personage catches the eye of David's mother, who is sitting by the fire feeling dismal.

I should explain a few more things. At the beginning of *David Copperfield*, David's mother is 'low in spirits' because she has no husband and any minute is expecting a baby. But David (who isn't even born yet) won't mind, because he has Peggotty. But Clara minds *very much*. She spends most of her time moping about and crying. 'Pull yourself together, pet,' says Maisie. 'Stop all that stuff and nonsense,' says Mum. 'Men simply aren't worth it.'

It is a windy afternoon in March when Betsey Trotwood marches up the garden path to visit her young widowed niece Clara Copperfield. Here is Betsey approaching the house:

> My mother had a sure foreboding at the second glance, that it was Miss Betsey. The setting sun was glowing on the strange lady, over the garden-fence, and she came walking up to the door with a fell rigidity of figure and composure of countenance that could have belonged to nobody else.
>
> (*David Copperfield*)

Betsey Trotwood arrives with the glowering sun. She arrives with 'fell rigidity of figure'. 'Full of bolsh,' Mum says. Betsey Trotwood is full of bolsh and bravado (that's being too sure of yourself). She walks up the garden path ramrod straight with her head held high. Above her head is the glowering sun.

Betsey Trotwood arrives like a change in the weather. But she's more than just the weather; she's a real mystery. Nobody knows where she has come from. She just arrives, suddenly, out of the blue, with no warning. No letter sent ahead, no telegram, no telephone call.

'It's all a bit much, really,' said Mum when the lady with the notepad came round.

But Betsey Trotwood comes with no notepad and pen. She arrives in a muddle and a stew, but then her whole history is a muddle. 'Here we go round the mulberry bush,' Mum says.

Betsey Trotwood once had a husband. That husband, who was very handsome, went to India to escape his wife.

People usually marry because they like the look of one another. But Betsey Trotwood's handsome husband clearly couldn't stand his wife. So he ran away to India where he took up the extravagant hobby of riding elephants and spent some time 'in the company of a Baboon'. Betsey's handsome husband left Betsey in the lurch. Margaret Thatcher's husband would never do that. Mum says that Denis Thatcher is as reliable as sliced white bread – what you see is what you get – whereas Betsey Trotwood's husband is quite unpredictable. 'A bit of a mystery,' says Maze. 'Nobody you'd want to rely on.'

But if you keep reading, it turns out that Betsey Trotwood's handsome husband *wasn't* seen in the company of a baboon, but with a 'baboo or begum'. A baboo or a begum are types of people, not monkeys. A baboo is a high-class Indian gentleman; a begum is a high-class Indian lady. In any case, by the time you've gone through all of that, you've stopped believing anyone about anything. It all sounds like a lot of nonsense. You might as well say that Betsey Trotwood's husband went off to join the circus. That the circus was in India is neither here nor there.

Still, the Formidable Personage has a definite reason for visiting: she's come to see the newborn baby. The trouble is David Copperfield hasn't been born yet, and Betsey Trotwood is cross about this. She wants to hold the baby and whisk him away. She likes babies; she wants to cuddle one. At least, she likes the idea of *this* baby. She's not really interested in anyone else.

'Why, bless my heart!' exclaimed Miss Betsey. 'You are a very Baby,' she says to David's mum. All Miss Betsey's comments are meant for babies, but because there aren't any babies at this point, Miss Betsey soon runs out of things to say.

So she turns her attention to the house, which is called The Rookery, and begins to complain about the name, which she thinks is silly. 'Where are the birds?' asks Miss Betsey, and looks out the window again. But as for the birds, you've got to admit Miss Betsey has a point. You shouldn't call a house The Rookery unless you've got some birds to show for it. Our house is called Grasmere, which is a place somewhere in the Lake District. Poets went there to rest and write and pray. William Wordsworth wrote 'Daffodils' there, which is Mum's favourite poem.

But all of this talk of names is delaying tactics. By now Betsey Trotwood is very agitated, and the trees outside begin to stir. *The evening wind made a disturbance just now, among some tall old elm-trees at the bottom of the garden, that neither my mother nor Miss Betsey could forbear glancing that way.*

All of this wind and disturbance is leading to something. Elm trees are dark and sinister. There are elm trees on the edge of the golf course near West beach; they are too tall for the rest of the space and they make everything around look flat and ugly. Whenever there's a storm they turn into screaming banshees. They lash and lash about, their necks flailing around so viciously I think they're going to snap. When I pass by on my bicycle, I hold my breath for fear they will lean down and grab me.

Whenever the wind whips around the windows my grandmother begins to get agitated. 'A storm is coming on,' says Maze. 'Close the window, dear. Push it down hard. Mind your fingers. For goodness' sake, put something under that gap. There's a dreadful wind coming through.'

Thankfully, a few pages later the doctor arrives. Mr Chillip (that's the doctor's name) goes upstairs to deliver the baby. But the baby takes a while in coming, and Betsey Trotwood becomes impatient again. She's restless. Poor Mr Chillip is made to feel ever so uncomfortable. Betsey Trotwood makes him feel that it's his fault. I'm sure he makes excuses to go upstairs more, to check on the baby, to avoid sitting by the fire with Betsey Trotwood, who keeps sighing and tutting away.

———————

Doctors were never seen in our house. Mum didn't believe in them and she wouldn't let us near hospitals, not since Great Aunt Matilda had been *butchered alive* on the surgeon's table in Worthing General at the turn of the century.

No, babies shouldn't be delivered by doctors but by midwives, and midwives were easy to come by if you just went a little further along the coast.

Two miles away on Sea Lane in Rustington was the Zachary Merton where babies were dragged from their mothers' bellies by women in brisk blue uniforms and white caps. Between

1968 and 1969 my grandmother was setting out on her bicycle along the sea front, past the retirement home, beyond the elm trees on the edge of the golf course, past the pebbled beach and the battered beach huts, before turning into Sea Lane towards the Zachary Merton and the strong arms and thighs of the matron, Cynthia Mary Grouse, who had once raised a farm full of albino goats. The Zachary Merton, Mum said, wasn't a hospital but a *maternity centre*; it was a place for women expecting babies *and nothing else*. She meant doctors; there were only matrons, and no doctors at the Zachary Merton; and then there was Maze, who was an *auxiliary*, and auxiliaries help matrons and matrons have long strong arms.

The Zachary Merton came from Africa. It belonged to a man called Zachary who everyone called Zach. Zach had decided it was safer to deliver babies by the sea in England than on the coast in Africa. In Africa, elephants and baboons might get at them and carry them away into the jungle; Zachary Merton knew of a baboon that had stolen a blond child and brought it up on banana leaves and mongoose. After a year, the child started to grow long dark hair and speak gibberish. Gone to the devil, said the locals, godless, forsaken. So Zachary the African, who was a good Christian man and came from a place called Moab, moved the Zachary Merton to Rustington on Sea where he painted it pearly white and planted palm trees around it to keep out the pesky flies. But there weren't many flies in Rustington on Sea, even in the summer, so Zachary Merton from Moab took down the palm trees and planted some elms because the locals told him they would withstand the pull of the salty wind. And Zachary Merton stayed in Rustington on Sea for many years; for long enough to see many blond babies born to healthy mothers – and without a single doctor in sight.

———————

Hours pass and Mr Chillip the doctor is forced to sit with Betsey Trotwood in the front parlour. Betsey Trotwood insists on keeping cotton wool in her ears to keep out the screams coming from upstairs.

Mr Chillip's view is that this 'unknown woman of portentous appearance' is quite a mystery. Why on earth is she here, and where does she come from? This is what we are all thinking. But Betsey Trotwood doesn't hear any of our thinking. She just carries on warming herself by the fire with cotton wool in her ears.

'Stubborn is as stubborn does,' Maisie says. Finally, after a lot of noise from upstairs, and a lot of pacing to and fro from Betsey Trotwood, the baby comes. The screaming upstairs stops; the murder is over.

———————

Mum tells me that I was born at six o'clock in the morning on a Monday or a Tuesday. She can't quite remember now. I was born in my mother's bed, not at the Zachary Merton. My brothers were born there instead. On the morning of 29 August 1972 I rolled over onto my mother's white sheets in her double bed and went straight to sleep. 'Well, we won't be having any trouble from her,' sniffed Cynthia Mary Grouse, and packed up her stiff black bag and left.

———————

'Well, Ma'am, I am happy to congratulate you,' says Mr Chillip, bounding downstairs. But happy Mr Chillip doesn't yet know what danger he is in. 'I am happy to congratulate you,' he says blithely, grinning from ear to ear no doubt.

'And *she*? How is *she*?' says Miss Betsey Trotwood, *sharply*. Mr Chillip looks confused.

'The baby,' said my aunt. 'How is she?'

Then Mr Chillip lets it slip. 'Ma'am … I apprehended you had known. It's a boy.' Poor Mr Chillip; he doesn't know what's hit him.

My aunt never said a word, but took her bonnet by the strings, in the manner of a sling, aimed a blow at Mr. Chillip's head with it, put it on bent, walked out, and never came back. She vanished like a discontented fairy, or like one of those supernatural beings whom it was popularly supposed I was entitled to see, and never came back any more.

Poor Mr Chillip. For a man to be bashed around the head by a bonnet somehow seems worse than being bashed around the head by a saucepan, which might really hurt. Being bashed around the head by a bonnet is just very silly and rather surprising. 'Foolish,' says Maze. 'Just plain foolish.'

But before anyone can say another thing, Betsey Trotwood disappears like *a discontented fairy*. Whoosh! Whoosh!

12

HAND-ME-DOWN
HISTORIES

The governess had run away two months before; and for all
Mr. Rochester sought her as if she had been the most precious
thing he had in the world, he never could hear a word of her;
and he grew savage – quite savage on his disappointment: he
never was a wild man, but he got dangerous after he lost her
… He broke off acquaintance with all the gentry, and shut
himself up like a hermit at the Hall.

(Jane Eyre)

Some people have special powers for disappearing. Betsey
Trotwood does, and so does Jane Eyre. All the characters I
read about – all the ones I liked, at least – seemed to disappear
into thin air.

When Jane Eyre leaves Thornfield Hall she disappears like
a sprite in the night. She isn't seen for years. When Jane Eyre
runs away, Mr Rochester spends months and months search-
ing for her, tracing the forests wild. I think that's what people
do when they go mad over love. They start running around
the woods looking for fairies.

By the rivers of Babylon, there we sat down,
Ye-eah we wept, when we remembered Zion

That's a song by Boney M. But Zion is just another name for the past, and when I think of the past I remember the records we played. I see those black circles spinning me around and around until I'm lying on the front-room floor feeling dizzy and sick.

'That's enough now,' says Mum, coming out from behind her bedroom door after lunch (it's always after lunch when Mum comes out). 'I've heard quite enough of that now. Can't you find something else to play?'

But it was Roger who gave us that record, Roger who came to our house with the people in stripy clothes, Roger who left us records, Roger who sang 'By the Rivers of Babylon' with his guitar on his knee, Roger who held hands with all of the wailing people of Babylon.

And Roger came with Sue, the Sue that everyone talks about but pretends not to know, the Sue who ran away, so they say. Roger came with Sue, so Roger must have known. Roger held hands with everyone: with Mum and Maze and my aunt and a man called Peter and a woman called Cynthia. Once upon a time everyone held hands and sang ring-a-ring-of-roses. Once upon a time a striking dark-haired woman sat on the floor of a house by the sea and told everyone that God was coming through the window any minute now and that they should hold hands nicely and say their prayers. So they did.

Sue held Roger's hand, round and round the garden like a teddy bear until they felt hot and dizzy from the singing. Then Sue led Roger into the garden and they sat down on the dry grass and stroked the rose petals and lifted them up towards the sky. Sue opened her hands and let the petals fall over her head and they lay back on the grass and closed their eyes and dreamed of Zion.

It was Sue who led Roger away: away from the people strumming guitars in the kitchen, the people wandering down the hallway, the people sitting in the front room cross-legged speaking Greek, the people Mummy holds hands with too, the people The Woman Upstairs beckons in through the back door with her bony finger, the people Maisie brings tea to on a tray, the people who sit around and whisper prayers to King David hoping he will come back down to earth: those people, the people praying for Zion.

But Zion is over the hill and far away, and for Zion to come, you have to lift your face unto the Lord.

———————

When you tell a story, at some point you have to move backwards. You can't just keep ploughing on. Things won't make sense otherwise, not to you nor to anyone. You have to know that the reason things are the way they are now is because other things happened before.

'Before you came along things were quite different,' Mum says mysteriously. '*Quite* different, young lady. Things weren't always as they are now.'

Miss Marple knows this. She knows that before the vicar married Greta things were very different indeed. For one thing, there was a lot less talk of detective fiction. But when you think about it, most stories are about what happened before: before Noah's Flood, before Eve ate the apple, before my aunt moved in, before the wailing people came to our house, before David died, before Sue Blunt disappeared, before the body was found in the vicar's study, before Mary the maid screamed, before Letitia Blacklock acquired the lump on her neck. But then, if none of that had happened, we wouldn't have anything to talk about. It's just annoying always being the person who comes after.

———————

Sometime before I was born Mum had been a seamstress. You only learn about the past in bits and pieces, when someone is in the mood to tell you. Mum told me things over a cup of coffee in the morning when she sat down to eat her crust. Every morning Mum ate a wafer of crusty bread with some butter on it. She liked bread without much bread in it, just the crusty part, the edge of the bread, the edge of the rocks where the knobbly faces jutted out. I watched Mum eating her crust and the rock folded flat in two.

While she was drinking her coffee, Mum told me that she used to make clothes for money. She had an old sewing machine called Singer but she did a lot by hand. Mum liked to say that she *did things by hand*. Doing things by hand included making embroderie anglaise.

Mum was so good at embroderie anglaise I imagined she had a job repairing the Bayeux Tapestry. A long time ago Mum went to France on a ferry. She took her sewing machine with her. Mum was sailing to France because she'd been asked by the kings and queens of Normandy to make a picture of them all out hunting. The French kings and queens wanted their picture to be as pretty as possible; they wanted their picture surrounded with roses.

Mum loved sewing embroderie anglaise. She put it all over my clothes. Embroderie anglaise was the pretty flowers she sewed onto the bottom of clothes; embroderie anglaise are flowers that grow along an old hem. Embroderie anglaise can cover up a multitude of sins. Skirts that are suddenly too short, dry and tattered hems.

But they don't need much water, Mum says. You want to make sure they keep their shape. Too much water is as bad as too little. Roses must grow together, with small spaces in between.

Embroderie anglaise is the part of the garden that lines up in rows, the back of the wall where Mum runs her roses. Her roses are still young now, but one day they will grow up to be beautiful young ladies: Mary and Constance and Eveline.

'Mary, Mary, quite contrary, how does your garden grow? With silver bells and cockle shells and pretty maids all in a row, a row, with pretty maids all in a row.'

Broderie anglaise, Mum said, was what the French king, William, sent to the English queen, Matilda, in order to win her over. When Matilda ran her fingers over the little pink and red ripples and the tiny blue and white crosses on the sea, she smiled and said, 'Oui.'

———————

Every story has a backstory. This is my backstory, but it's not really mine, if you know what I mean. It's what Mum calls *making do*. Making do is sewing over the bare parts of clothes around the elbows and knees. Sometimes it means adding another layer to the hem. Then it becomes a hand-me-down. History is full of hand-me-down projects.

Sometime before I was born there was a tall flint tower overlooking the sea. Some people say it was Norman, others that it was Saxon, but the tower had stood strong and sturdy for hundreds of years. One day in the 1970s – I can't say which year exactly – a queen came to live in our long, thin house by the sea. Suddenly our house had a tower. The tower had a flag on top that faced out towards the sea.

The queen brought a subject with her. He was her only subject. The queen had lost all her other subjects. The subject's name was David, but after a while he was sent away too, because the queen didn't think he was a suitable subject and he would certainly never make a king. So the queen went to live in the tower alone. She disappeared behind the white door in the tower and didn't come out for years.

Then one day the tower fell into the sea. No one knows how this happened, but the story goes that one night a fire broke out on top. The floor was rickety and old and some candles had been left burning. The people in the tower lit candles when they sang their songs, but when the Spirit of God moved among them, they forgot the candles lying on the floor. And the flames crept through the orange and brown carpet and swallowed it whole.

———————

History is full of sad queens and aunts. See Queen Victoria after Prince Albert died. She sailed off to the Isle of Wight and refused to get the ferry back. With no queen on the throne, England was scuppered.

Then there is the sad history of Betsey Trotwood. After she heard the news of her handsome husband's death, she went off to live in a tiny place by the sea. This is the history of Betsey Trotwood according to David Copperfield:

> From India, tidings of his death reached home, within ten years. How they affected my aunt, nobody knew; for immediately upon the separation, she took her maiden name again, bought a cottage in a hamlet on the sea-coast a long way off, established herself there as a single woman with one servant, and was understood to live secluded, ever afterwards, in an inflexible retirement.

> (*David Copperfield*)

After all this, Betsey goes into exile. It isn't true that nobody knew how she felt about the news. Of course they knew. They just didn't want to know. Anyone who moves to a cottage far away by the sea can hardly be rejoicing. You move away because you don't want anyone you know to see your tears.

And then there is the story of Jane Eyre. Thorough bush thorough brier Jane Eyre moves away too. After the scene at the altar, after Mr Rochester goes mad with disappointment, after the ghastly woman upstairs is discovered and comes downstairs, after her wedding veil is torn in two, Jane knows there is no staying, so she flees.

Early one morning, she stows herself away inside a coach with a small parcel of belongings. She leaves Thornfield Hall and its turrets and tower behind her. She leaves Mr Rochester slumped asleep on a chair outside her room, Mr Rochester, desperate and alone. She leaves! She leaves because she must. Her soul has told her so. *Let me be torn away!* Like Cinderella, she orders the carriage.

And the carriage takes her to a town called Whitcross where she finds a stone pillar pointing four ways. Now she must decide which way to go. But just as the carriage pulls away she realises that she has left her small parcel behind. Without that parcel she is *absolutely destitute* and *alone*.

So she strikes out across the heath. Starved and sodden, she sees, in the distance, a village and spire. She stumbles into the village and spies a shop. A baker's! Hot dough! She can almost feel it on her tongue. Fresh bread rears up in front of her, delicious and warm. She asks the shopkeeper for a bun, but the lady with the pinafore tied round her waist says no. *We can't have ragamuffins like you coming in here and asking for free loaves of bread. Keep your filthy hands off! Now out you go!*

Almost dead with hunger, Jane arrives at a cottage door. She knocks and a servant answers, a woman with a suspicious look. Before the woman can close the door on her, Jane falls across the threshold. Moments later, she is scooped up by a tall, handsome man with a Greek face who carries her inside.

This is the beginning of a new Jane, a Jane with new relatives. And so exit Jane Eyre of Thornfield Hall with the tall, dark tower.

PART TWO

13

AUNT JAYNE

This might surprise you, but I had another aunt, called Jayne (with a 'y'), my younger aunt who came to visit when the sun came out. She was Aunt Jayne who came down in the summer. Aunt Jayne was ten years younger than my other aunt. She was the whoopsie-daisy sister.

The first thing you need to know about Aunt Jayne is that she had a boyfriend and his name was Bill.

'Fancy that!' said Maze, who loved Aunt Jayne because Aunt Jayne always brought presents. 'Fancy that, coming all that way on the train, with all those things. Such extravagance, Jayne. Really, you shouldn't. You should save your money for *better things*. What on earth does Bill say?'

But Aunt Jayne never went into what Bill might say – Uncle Bill, she called him – because no one wanted to know what Bill had to say and her words would have been wasted.

Uncle Bill only came down at Christmas, and then he sat in the corner of the front room and ate a Toblerone: a long pyramid-shaped tunnel of chocolate running through the Alps.

'The Swiss have to build their tunnels through the mountains to get anywhere. You've got to get around mountains in

Switzerland. Broom-broom … right on through.'

Uncle Bill snapped off a piece of the chocolate tunnel and handed it to me. 'Don't tell the grown-ups. Never tell the grown-ups anything. They're not fun.' Uncle Bill had a voice that fell down quietly at the end. His words mashed slightly at the end, because Uncle Bill was Irish and Irish people speak with a lilt said Maze.

'Sing-song … their words go up and down, up and down, over the hills and far away. Now really, Bill, don't you have better things to spend your money on than big blocks of Toblerone?'

Better things was food and milk, school shoes, summer sandals, the electricity bill; better things was fresh eggs, bread, and proper minced meat. For Aunt Jayne, better things was getting some sun on your limbs.

'Children in England look like uncooked pastry,' Aunt Jayne pronounced to whoever was listening. 'Let's get some sun on those limbs.'

Aunt Jayne believed in picnics and ice cream and sunbathing. A picnic meant a rug, sandwiches wrapped in tin foil with thick cheese, chocolate fingers, and fresh strawberries. So Aunt Jayne scooped us up – my brothers, three cousins and me – and took us down to the beach. Before we left the house she made sure that we all had our swimming costumes on under our clothes, 'to avoid any beach embarrassment', she said, because Aunt Jayne was a real lady. She knew what should be kept in and what out. 'Tummies and bottoms in, shoulders out.'

'Naked bits,' said my brother Peter. 'No naked bits on the beach. We're not perverts! No one's to see our naked bits. Perverts will, though. Perverts live to see naked bits!'

Perverts were hard to spot because they were always brown. They blended in. Perverts lay out in the sun all day turning brown. Not a single part of a pervert's body remained white because perverts wore no clothes. They even sat down to eat their corn flakes in the nude.

'That must be a bit tricky if they ever had an accident,' said Maze.

'Perverts poo all over themselves,' said my younger brother Michael.

'I meant if they ever dropped any food over themselves. Hot soup wouldn't be very nice, never mind corn flakes,' said Maze.

When Aunt Jayne took us to the beach we had to make sure that nobody thought we were perverts. This was difficult for me, because my swimming costume was made from crochet. Anybody and everybody, if they wanted to, could see right through it, right through to everything!

Crochet is a kind of knitting, but with lots of holes. Crochet is French and means 'hook'. To crochet you need a sharp needle with a hook at the top. To crochet is to thread one stitch through another. When you crochet you pass one stitch across, back and through and behind another. When you crochet you create gaps big enough to poke your fingers through.

Crochet lets in a lot of air, and that's why Mum liked it so much. Mum was fond of aired bodies.

'Nicely aired now, nice and open. You want everything open to the air, in the summer. Toes and tummies!'

'But not fannies,' my brother said. 'Never ever show your fanny.'

Mum liked us to wear open-toed sandals to the beach. Jesus-creepers we called them, horrible, embarrassing Jesus-creepers. No one wore Jesus-creepers, only people with coloured clothes and long hair, people who sang about Jesus with stars in their eyes.

Nobody wore Jesus-creepers. Nobody! Nobody! Nobody! We told Mum this but she wouldn't listen. Everyone wore trainers except us. Everyone, everyone, everyone!

Aunt Jayne didn't wear Jesus-creepers; she wore silvery sandals that dipped down towards the ground. Above her ankles sat a pretty hem. Aunt Jayne sailed out of our house with her cotton hem rippling across her calves. Aunt Jayne billowed. She set sail.

And she kept us out all day. The minute Aunt Jayne put a cardigan over her sundress we knew it was time to go home.

And when we got home, Mum was always there, sounding cross. 'Get back outside right now and hose yourselves down. I don't want you walking any more sand through the house.'

Sand always put Mum in a bad mood. She didn't seem to mind the rest: the layers and layers of carpet fluff or thick grease building up around the tiles; or the green mould lining the edges of the bath, so thick it resembled a pond; or the mildew hanging from the ceiling of the hallway; or the rotting wood along the windowpanes; or the rust stuck to the front-door latch, the rust around the lock, the rust that meant that several times a week we couldn't open the back garden gate and run down the twitten, the twitten where we were never really allowed.

A twitten, by the way, is an alleyway. Mum loved the word 'twitten'. If you went down the twitten you were likely to turn into a 'twit', another of Mum's favourite words. To be a twit was to behave as though your brain was switched off; a twit was someone who wasn't thinking; a twit was a twig and a twig could be blown away on a puff of wind; a twig would get stuck in your hair and you'd end up walking around with it in the back of your head all day without you knowing it was there. When that happened you really were a twit, and every-one could see it. To be honest, Jane Eyre is a bit of a twit when she leaves her bag behind in the carriage. Aunt Jayne was never a twit because she was slim and stylish and people looked at her when she passed by; Aunt Jayne lived in London and in London people had jobs and earned money. People who lived in London were rarely destitute and alone.

But Aunt Jayne wasn't always in the good books. She had a boyfriend and a boyfriend might lead to marriage and that was terrible. Look what happened to Betsey Trotwood – she married and it was a disaster. The handsome husband ran off to India and dragged her name through the mud. He was probably wearing a dhoti over there just to shame her. A dhoti, Mum said, was a cotton nappy, 'a very peculiar way to go on … practically savage'.

Marriage was the worst thing anyone could ever do. To be married was to be inside Mr Brocklehurst's burning pit. To be married was to be eaten alive by hot flames; flames licking up the flesh on your calves, your thighs, your arms, your neck, your hair. To be married was to be *immolated*, to be swallowed up whole by fire. This happens to widows in India after their husbands die. Women in India throw themselves on a bonfire after their husbands die. Of course Betsey Trotwood didn't do this. She had more sense.

No. After her husband died, Betsey Trotwood moved to a little village by the sea and began to keep donkeys. She took up with a man called Mr Dick, who, by the way, was never her boyfriend. Boyfriends and husbands are nothing but trouble, Mum says, it's bound to lead to a sticky end.

14

THE SILVER JUBILEE

Aunt Jayne was down the year of the Silver Jubilee. That was 1977, the year the queen sat in St Paul's Cathedral and lifted a golden sceptre up towards the sky. That summer, Aunt Jayne was wearing a pretty sundress and she was sitting close to the queen. I could hear them speaking.

Queen: Hello, dear, how are you? I do like your sundress, such a pretty pattern. Is it poppies? Yes, red poppies on a blue and white background. How refreshing! I can't get away with such a thing. They like me to cover my arms, you know. It's more refined. A queen isn't supposed to show off her arms.

Aunt Jayne: You could always try a shawl, a nice lacy one. Ange – she's my sister – makes a lovely bit of crochet. She could come up with something, quick as a flash, and then you wouldn't need to worry about your arms. You're still young, Your Majesty. And you have a lovely smile. That's all we'll be looking at, your beautiful, beaming, royal smile!

Then the queen looked at Aunt Jayne and smiled one of her bright-as-a-torch-at-midnight smiles. This young woman would make a very good lady-in-waiting, thought the queen.

'Now, Your Royal Highness, I do think this pale mauve might do you very well for your going-away dress.'

'But my dear, I'm not getting married. This is my Jubilee!'

'But Your Highness, it's nice to have something you can move well in. You don't want to be tripping over your own hem. It's better to have the hem sitting on the top of your ankles rather than on the bottom. And you want a little heel … Nothing too much, just enough to pick you up off those hard paving stones. They're so chilly on the bones.'

———————

Jubilee month was hot and sunny and people were eating strawberries at Wimbledon. Aunt Jayne was down and the front door sat on the latch.

'For goodness' sake, leave the door on the latch.' Mum was anxious. She was expecting a delivery. *Ding dong!*

The bell rang and we ran downstairs. Outside, a large cardboard box was sitting next to our lion. My brothers carried it upstairs.

'A television,' Mum said solemnly. We'd never seen a television before. It was small and black and grey and made of plastic. It didn't look like anything at all.

'I wanted the larger one, but it was out of our range. This is the best we can do,' Mum said.

We perched the black-and-grey square on an old coffee table in my aunt's room and fiddled with the aerial to try and tune it. But the channels kept fizzing in and out.

'Poor reception,' said Mum. 'We've got poor reception. I told the man in Curry's we needed a bigger aerial. There are a lot of us. I told him that. There are a lot of us to fit around and pass through. We need a bigger aerial. But they *never* listen, those men in those shops. You tell them what you want and they never, ever listen.'

We lay on the carpet in front of the small square box and waited for the fizzing to stop. Every time a breeze ran through the room the aerial flopped over and hung like a dead bird across the screen.

'For goodness' sake! Someone sit that thing down properly. Get some tape … use your brain … Tape it down to the back! It'll snap in two. It's all cheap plastic … nothing is ever properly made these days … everything *Made in China*, as if the Chinese have any idea what we in England require in our front room!'

———————

That June we lay like lizards with our stomachs pressed close to the floor and watched the queen glide down the nave of Westminster Abbey: the queen in black and white, the queen in 1953, the queen twenty-five years before, the queen going to get her crown.

All day long the queen was in black and white. I can't remember her in colour. I see her moving like a pretty ghost down a long, endless nave, with a smile fixed to her face as if it might fall off. Behind us I can hear my aunt's voice blaring out.

'Well, she's got her life set out for now, Ange, hasn't she? And she'll outlive Charles. Women always do. That woman will keep going until she's ninety … a hundred. You'll see. She looks like a sylph but she's built like an ox. That woman's going nowhere. Charles doesn't stand a chance. He's stiff as a ramrod. Look at him! I can't imagine him catching a girl, can you? Someone must have put him up to taking her on. There's not much natural passion there. They're all stiff in that family – stiff as a doorpost. No life in them except when they drink, I bet. But the queen's got her smile on right, you have to give her that. She's got that smile worked out, and that smile's going *nowhere*!'

'It's a pity it's in black and white,' said Mum. 'Takes away from the dress.'

'Twenty-six-inch waist. Small. Tiny really, a will-o'-the-wisp … nipped in. Well, they don't have time to eat, do they? It's all for show. Banquets and dinners. Nobody eats at those. They just pick at it. You raise your fork at the right moment and nod and smile.'

The queen wasn't doing much nodding today. She was perfectly still, like a statue, except when she was gliding and raising her rod. 'There she goes … up with the orb and sceptre, down with the crown. They must have to practise that a few times. That would take some doing. She must have some steel in her, that woman.'

The queen was one of those ships in the harbour with buoys hanging off her to keep her moored. Today, her crown was a bobbing buoy. I watched the crown lower slowly over her head. It took forever to reach the tip of her hair. It didn't look as if it would fit. It was too big. A puff of wind and it would blow right off out to sea.

'Must take hours of practice to sit that still,' said Mum.

'Deportment, Ange. All the Royals have deportment lessons. She'll have practised this countless times before. They'd have had several run-throughs ... nothing is left to chance. That's what being a Royal is all about. After all, you can't afford to get anything wrong for the telly, can you?'

Poor queen! She existed only for the telly. The queen was a tiny girl in black and white inside a small plastic box. I felt sorry for her. She looked very lonely sitting in Westminster Abbey with only old men around her, droopy old men who kept dropping things on her head.

'She must be very stiff now. She hasn't moved for hours,' I said.

'She goes right back to the Tudors and Plantagenets,' announced my aunt with her 'all of history' voice on. She was wrong: the queen went back to the House of Hanover in Germany. We'd done it at school with Mr Drake.

'The Tudors were the first great kings and queens of England. Henry VIII is in her blood. You can see it around the eyes. See, Ange – they're just a little piggy. The Tudors have small, piggy eyes ... mean eyes, red around the rim.'

I peered closely at the queen. I couldn't see any signs of a red beard or a bulging belly. Her eyes weren't small and piggy. The queen was small and pretty – petite, my grandmother said. The queen was *petite*. Her face was neat and pretty and tidied away like Miss Marple's best silver. The queen was definitely pretty. But it was a sensible sort of pretty. She didn't have time to spend in front of the mirror. The queen had to get on with things. Spit-spot. If you were the queen it didn't really matter how pretty you were, only how well you smiled and shook hands, and how well you could remember names. 'His Royal Highness of Eurasia'. That sort of thing. You probably had to remember huge long lists of names, names of people you'd never see again.

But you had to greet them well, shake their hand firmly but graciously and ask them how their trip had been across the Indian Ocean. Had they managed to catch forty winks? Except you wouldn't put it like that. You'd ask His Royal Highness of Eurasia if he was well rested and then you'd ask after his family, whose names you'd also have to know. Then you'd wish you'd written them all down. The queen must carry bits of paper in her handbag with lists of names written on them. She must have a special names-only notebook which her ladies-in-waiting keep up to date like Mum's Special Numbers at the back of her diary.

Finally, after an age, the queen went out into the crowds to wave.

'Why doesn't she walk about a bit?' said my cousin. 'Isn't she allowed?'

'She might get shot,' said my brother Michael. 'Then there'd be blood everywhere and the police would have to come with guns and there'd be more shooting and the queen would have to throw herself into a bush, and then we'd see up her dress, and all the camera men would be snooping around taking pictures *up the queen's dress*, and the next day the newspapers would be full of pictures of the queen's knickers and the queen's bum stuck inside a bush.'

'And she'd miss lunch,' piped up my cousin.

'Pack it in, you lot, we can't hear the commentary. There'll be no such thing! The queen has bodyguards, hired guards. They'll be swarming all over the place like ants.'

'They should be disguised as birds,' said my middle brother. 'Or bats.'

'Bats and mice,' I said. 'Voles.'

'Big black crows,' said my brother.

'Shh! Pack it in! We can't hear a thing!'

'There's nothing to hear,' I said. 'Only the crowd cheering.'

'Shh! I want to hear the commentary. They might read some poetry or something in the Poets' Corner. William Wordsworth is buried there, you know, Dice. Oh, I do hope someone does a nice "Daffodils".'

'If the queen got shot, who would take over?' asked my brother.

'Shh! The queen is not going to get shot. Pack it in and listen. They're about to start. I want to hear the words – "*Beside the lake, beneath the trees, fluttering and dancing in the breeze … when all at once I saw a crowd, a host of golden daffo-dils.*" Look, the archbishop is getting up to read. He's got a lovely reading voice … chocolatey, like Sinatra.'

15

THE BEACH HOTEL

I haven't said much about men so far because men never stayed very long in our house. Men came and went, came and went, like gadflies, but when Mum said *Sinatra* she meant the man we called Laurie.

What do I know about Laurie? Well, that Laurie is short for Laurence. Maze told me that. And Laurie is the man standing at the back door the day David went missing. Laurie is the man going away in the ambulance. Laurie is the man with a pink bleary face; Laurie is the man going bald; Laurie is the man in the photo with my pink sausage dog between his legs. Laurie is the man with long gangly legs and arms and a thick Scottish accent. Laurie is the man who says 'pet' a lot, and Laurie is my dad.

Laurie had another wife once called Nadine. That was before all this. Nadine liked to shout and scream and I think she liked to drink. Sometimes she ran around with a knife and that's when the real trouble began.

According to my aunt, Laurie and Nadine used to row all the time. Night after night the saucepan went flying, and then one night, a very bad night, Laurie ended up with a knife in his back. It was because of that knife that Dad ran away from Eastbourne and his grotty flat to find Zion.

It was Maze who first told him about Zion: Zion, she said, meaning 'pure in heart'. Zion: those waiting for the Kingdom of God to come; those people who came to Lancing on Sea in 1969 looking for The Lady Who Knew God. It was in Zion that Mum met Dad sitting cross-legged on the carpet with his mouth wide open and his hands in the air.

———————————

But once upon a time, before I was born, things were very different between Mum and Dad. Once upon a time, Dad was in love with Mum, and this is the story Maze told me in between the washing up.

It is Saturday night in 1969 and Mum is dressed up to go out. She's been getting ready for hours. Her blonde hair sits in neat circles on the top of her lacy dress; her pink frilly shoes sit close together. Clutching her black leather handbag close to her waist, Mum trembles and lifts the curtain.

The occasional car goes by. She'd better stay here, she thinks. She might miss him if she stands by the door. Her shoes pinch. She should sit down for as long as she can; fold her legs beneath her and hold in the fright.

A car hoots and Mum jumps. She opens her bag to check for her purse. Snap. She checks for the note. Just about enough. Snap. She stands up and smooths down her skirt. She knows a lady never wears creases. She will be home by ten thirty.

'Laurie,' she said to Maze. 'He's called Laurie.'

'Laurence with a "u" or a "w"?' Maze asks.

'With a "u".'

'With a "u". Friendlier. Not a Lawrence of Arabia.'

Hoot. Hoot. Mum runs out. Inside the car she remembers she has forgotten her scarf.

'It'll be cold along the pier. You'll get a chill.'

Never mind. They can go inside for a coffee. Mum likes coffee, coffee with cream. She likes to watch it pour.

'Marilyn Monroe,' he said. 'You look like Marilyn Monroe in *Some Like it Hot*.'

There is another story about Mum and Dad, less sweet; for a tiny while Mum thought about marriage. The evening on the pier had turned serious; the man from Glasgow had won her heart. Mum had on her dress, her frilly white heels, her Bo-peep handbag, her special Lancôme scent. On the morning of her wedding she clutched a posy of pink roses to her breast.

But something got in the way, and that morning Mum found herself, like Jane Eyre, stranded at the altar. As the minister asked does anyone here, there came a piercing scream. Heads turned. At the back of the church a dark-haired woman was screaming 'No! No! No!' Mum dropped her roses and ran. The Woman Upstairs was at the back of the church, screaming.

When someone starts to scream, things move fast. Frilly pink shoes scuttle. Faces turn towards the church door and back again. The man at the altar hangs his head. His arms go limp.

Paper rustles. Handbags open looking for sweets and tissues. The man at the altar sits down on the stone floor and begins to weep.

Outside the church Mum clings to her roses, but a head of dark hair pushes her into a car. Mum grips the roses tighter; their petals flutter to the ground. Dark hair climbs in beside her and fills the rear window; the car pulls away. The man on the stone floor lies face-down and weeps.

The seagulls screamed especially loud that day, so the story goes.

———————

But then one day he was there again, coming through the back door, the man with no hair and a strange accent. It was 14 February, Valentine's Day, and the man Mum called Laurie had come to take her out.

'The children are coming along too, Laurie. I'm not playing silly games. None of us needs to be wined and dined, we just need to know what you're up to. You've been away for nearly two years. Two years is a long time. For a child, it's an eternity. And now you whisk in here and you want to go out for dinner. Do you know what we eat most nights? Cheese on toast, or nothing at all!'

The row went on for a while. I pressed my ear to the door and I heard Mum huffing and puffing like an angry wolf and behind the door I could see her face steaming red and the man with no hair pacing up and down. By the time they came out it was dark and we were getting dressed to go out to the Beach Hotel.

'Sally, put on your dress with the green collar and velvet hem. I don't want you looking like a ragamuffin. Peter, tuck your shirt in, for goodness' sake! Right, coats on, and do them up! We're going to a nice hotel. I want you to look your best. Paul, go and wash your face. You've got a nasty black streak on your chin.'

The Beach Hotel was on the other side of the main road behind a long stone wall; around the front and sides grew dark elm trees and pines. 'Tall lords and ladies,' said Maze, who knew all her trees.

I thought of Betsey Trotwood. She wouldn't have been happy with the name 'Beach Hotel'. It was too far from the beach to call it that. No, Betsey Trotwood would have sent a cross note to the manager to let him know that if he had any sort of sensible ideas in his head he would have called the hotel Pine Tree Lodge or The Elms.

'If you had any practical ideas of life, sir, you would know that you don't call a thing what it is not. If you are expecting a boy you don't call him Emily. If you are, however, you might call him David. When you are on more certain terms, you might call him Davy, but only after a lot of fuss and hulla-balloo. In the name of Heaven! There'll only be cause for disturbance, and much complaint.'

And then I thought of Miss Marple. She would have been cross about the lack of a sea view.

'Well really, Dolly. I do call this a bit much, don't you? I can't see beyond that dirty streetlamp, let alone the beach.' Miss Marple looked at her companion who wasn't paying any attention at all, only pulling at the curtains. 'Can you see anything, Dolly dear? And did you bring your binoculars?'

'Of course I did, Jane. Stop fussing. Here, let me have a look. If I can't see anything through these then I'm going to *insist* that we are moved. This is distinctly *not* a sea view! Now Jane, move that chair. I want to get closer to the window. And be a dear and tuck those curtains away for a moment. I need to get a proper look. Shabby ... I call this quite shabby.'

Dolly lifted her leg firmly onto the chair by the window. The chair wobbled. 'Jane, will you give me a lift up? Come on dear, like we used to at school ... Hand over thumb and up ... now ... lift-off! Mind my nylons!'

But the Beach Hotel had always been hidden from the sea, behind a lovely sea wall, Mum said, Sussex flint. The Beach Hotel was surrounded by Sussex and hidden by stone. I'd never seen the hotel from the front, and I would never have dared go up the wide stone steps, or through the glass doors, if Mum hadn't been pushing me hard from behind.

'Mum!'

I felt her handbag digging into my back. 'Go on! In you go. Straight ahead, down the hall.'

But the hall was dark, and except for a few peach lampshades stuck to the wall, I couldn't see anything. I stopped and looked and blinked. 'Go on!' Mum said from behind. 'Hurry up! We haven't got all day!'

A man with dark skin appeared from the peach light; he smiled and white teeth split through his brown skin. I jumped back, but Mum tut-tutted and pushed me forward towards a round table with a white candle sitting in a circle of plastic flowers. Christmas decorations, I thought, but it isn't Christmas. I looked around. There was no one here but us.

'There's no one here but us! Where is everyone? This is too weird.'

'Sit down, young lady, and do as you're told. Remember your manners. No one wants to hear your booming voice. We're in a restaurant, and this is a hotel. Now shh!'

I climbed onto a plastic chair and yelped. The plastic was cold and the legs squeaked. Peter and Paul grinned and sank slowly down the backs of their chairs. Michael clung to Mum's hand.

'Shh!' Mum said, frowning. 'And sit up straight. Stop slouching, for goodness' sake!'

I could see the lines on her face in the candlelight. Dad was sitting opposite, scratching his head and looking nervous. Mum was about to launch into one of her speeches again. He put his hands on the table and turned them over and over.

'Well, Laurie, what are you planning to do? The children need new clothes … Peter's shooting up like a beanpole … I don't have enough on the child benefit.'

Talk of benefits was a bad sign, and Mum's face was steaming up.

'I get £68 a week, Laurie, for everything. Michael is starting school this September. He'll need a uniform.'

'I can't go back to the Zachary Merton, Angela, not after Saudi. I didn't qualify.'

'Well, we can't go on like this, Laurie, can we?'

When Mum started her 'can we's I knew there was trouble. Her face went white as a ghost and her lips thin. Dad stared out across the table, into blank space. He was beginning to regret the whole thing.

'Can I take your order?' The man with brown skin was standing with a notepad and grinning again.

'What would you like to order, dear?' Dad looked at Mum.

'Dear, is it? Well … we'd like grapefruit for starters and then the chicken for the main. The children can eat grapefruit and bread and butter.'

'Perhaps some hot soup, madam?'

'Soup is for convalescents and old people. The children will do fine with the starter. Thank you.'

Maze sometimes ate grapefruit in the mornings, sprinkled with brown sugar. No one ate grapefruit at night.

'Grapefruit? For dinner?'

'Shh! You'll do what you're told. It's a special treat.'

The grinning man came back with a white napkin thrown over his shoulder.

'Fresh grapefruit from the morning market.'

'I don't suppose that is true,' said Mum with her thin lips on. 'But never mind, grapefruit is grapefruit. It's very refreshing.'

'You can't get grapefruit in Saudi, Angela.'

'What a shame, Laurie. Worth coming back for, then!'

I stuck my spoon in and the grapefruit jumped. It flipped across the table and smacked my brother Michael in the face.

'Ahhhh! Ahhhh! Ahhh! It's freezing … it's freezing cold.'

'Pack it in! Pack it in all of you. That noise is disgraceful! This is a special treat, coming out like this. I think you need to go home right away. You don't have the manners for sitting out in a restaurant. I'm ashamed of you. You're behaving like animals! Laurie and I are talking!'

'No you're not.' Peter was in a bad mood now. 'You're not talking at all.'

'Right, I think it's time you all went home. Peter, take yourself home … take all of them home. Sally, you too. Hold Michael's hand across the road. Get yourselves into your pyjamas and straight into bed.'

'Can we make some toasted cheese?'

'No! Straight to bed. All of you!'

'We can't eat the grapefruit. It's frozen, and it's too cold to eat. Who eats grapefruit at night?' Peter slammed his spoon down on the table.

'Right! Off, now! All of you!'

So we left our freezing-cold grapefruit behind and crossed the main road in the dark.

The next morning Mum told us that Dad had gone back to Saudi Arabia to find money.

16

A MURDER IS ANNOUNCED

People kill for money, even genteel ladies. Mum would say it's the devil in her, but once you start, you can't stop. Murder is a runaway train.

Genteel ladies are usually kind. Letitia Blacklock in *A Murder is Announced* is kind to her old friend Dora Bunner, but Letitia Blacklock doesn't quite trust Bunny, because Bunny has a way of letting things slip.

Poor Bunny! The trouble is that she can only remember Letitia Blacklock as Lotty, her school friend Charlotte Blacklock. Once upon a time they held hands and walked around the village together. They were inseparable. 'Just like an old couple,' said Mrs Blount, the postmistress. 'Inseparable … when they grow up they'll probably marry!' So, no matter how hard she tries, Bunny can't erase Lotty Blacklock.

But she must try harder! Lotty is now Letty: Letty Blacklock, Letitia Blacklock, the woman who will inherit her father's estate, the woman who has *no* huge goitre (lump) on her neck; the woman who *doesn't* have to wear a large pearl necklace in order to hide her ugly past, her ruined future.

Sometimes it's easier to announce a murder in a newspaper; that way you can put people off the scent and turn it into a game. Then the whole village begins to play.

In Chipping Cleghorn, where Letitia Blacklock lives, everyone knows it's Johnnie Butt who delivers the papers. Every morning, except Sunday, Johnnie pushes a copy of the *Telegraph*, *The Times*, the *Daily Mail* and the local *Gazette* through the front door of Little Paddocks, where Letitia Blacklock and her old friend Dora Bunner are having breakfast with Miss Blacklock's naughty nephew and niece, Patrick and Julia. In Chipping Cleghorn, people read the *Gazette* mainly for the announcements; they read them because it is the quickest way to learn something about the contents of their neighbours' houses, their habits and routines, their obsessions.

That morning, the morning of 29 October (1949, let's say), Dora Bunner suddenly spies, among the offers of used Morris Minors and old Daimlers, garden equipment and pleas for a better maid, an announcement of murder. Lotty look, look, look at this!

A murder is announced and will take place on Friday, October 29th, at Little Paddocks at 6.30 p.m. Friends please accept this, the only intimation.

(*A Murder is Announced*)

'Well, blow me down!' my aunt screeched one afternoon. 'Listen to this, Ange: *"We can do business together": Margaret Thatcher strikes business deal with Mikhail Gorbachev.* Dressed like that she certainly can. That's a smart woman – she knows what she's doing, facing Russia in red and gold. Ange, look at this. Thatcher dressed like a tin soldier!'

Mum glanced up from her coffee. She looked weary and pale.

'"*It's a deal!*" she says. She's a good businesswoman, Thatcher. Listen to this, Ange: "*I like Mr Gorbachev.*" Well, perhaps not "*like*" … she needs to be careful with her terms of affection, Ange. You don't want to emphasise that point too hard. Not with the Russians. They have dark souls. You can't really *like* a Russian, Ange, can you? No, I don't think "like" is quite what she means. What she means is *perestroika!*'

My aunt pronounced the word and it sounded like a firework going off. We jumped.

'*Perestroika!* Do you know what that is, Ange?'

Mum blinked. 'Remind me, Dice. I've written it down somewhere, but I can't quite recall. I get all those Russian words muddled. '*Perestroika … Lebensraum.* What's the other one … *glas-y-nost?*'

'Openness!' My aunt grinned. 'She's going to open up Russia to itself. Throw open the doors, make things transparent, brush away the cobwebs, force them out of their corrupt and seedy ways. Russia is steeped in corruption. Those Communists muttering in dark corners … the secret police, plots, plots, plots. Remove the taint of Stalin, the mass murderer. Exorcise a few demons. It's about time too that Russia got to grips with its murky past.'

'But which is which, Dice? Which is for Russia, and which for Germany? I can't remember. Which words are for which place? I'm in a muddle … I can never quite remember … they move *about* so much.'

———————

The newspaper was a serious business in my house. After reading it out loud in her reading voice, my aunt sat on her bed with her legs folded and cut out the most important articles, then stuck them carefully in her scrapbook. With a blue ballpoint pen she scrawled dates over the top of the headlines. March 1979, February 1980, January 1981, winter 1983, spring 1984. *Arthur Scargill in busted anorak; Michael Heseltine has his hair done; trade unions set to ruin the nation; Thatcher tells naughty boys to stop messing about; Arthur Scargill on blowy hillside in Barnsley; Nigel Lawson turns us all posh; Denis Thatcher: handbag holder; Morning Margaret tells Denis to put the toast on; Denis holds her handbag wrong; Wet, wet and wetter; Thatcher: holding out for a hero.*

Snip, snip, snip, her scissors went through the paper. Soon the newspaper was a mass of oblongs and squares. With a quick dab of glue she pressed the oblongs and squares tightly between her blue and purple pages. Snap! And the drawbridge went down, the page turned over, the lid was closed, and all the documents of the newspaper world were stored away inside my aunt's paper castle.

GIRL WITH DOVE

When one book was filled she sent us to the newsagent's to get another.

'It must be blue and purple,' she announced loudly. 'Blue and purple … the colours of the papacy and the monarchy. If you're going to keep documents, you need to give them a proper home! Now off you go, I'm a day behind as it is!'

After a while, her scrapbooks became too fat to slip beneath her bed. Then she called for one of us. 'Hey, one of you, come here now! I need some help with my scrapbook. Get under the bed and push it towards me. I need to look something up … No, that side, *that* side. You can't get at it from there, for goodness' sake!'

And so one of us crawled around the side of her dusty bed through cigarette ash and bits of old tissue to push her bulging book from behind.

'Careful! I don't want anything torn! There's important history in there … history in the making! Keep your dirty little hands out of there!'

───────────

It was at London University in the 1960s that my aunt learned to document. This is what she told Mum anyway; Mum, who believed everything she said.

'Everything happened in the sixties, Ange. Everything. If you weren't in London in the sixties you missed one of the great moments in World History.'

'But I wasn't there, Dice. I was here in Sussex. I was taking my art class.'

— 110 —

'Well, never mind. The point is that one of us was. I was there and I can tell you all about it now. But you really had to be there. I mean really be there, be in the thick of it, all that energy swirling about waiting to land … I was just so glad to be there, right there, Ange, when it all came through.'

At London University, my aunt sat down in a quiet library with tweezers and white gloves and carefully turned the pages of Tudor letters. The pages were as thin as old skin, as thin as Elizabeth I's skin when she was very old (she died aged sixty-nine, I think, which for back then was more like ninety-nine).

The Tudors loved secrets; they liked to poke and pry. Poking and prying was what Cardinal Wolsey did best, because Wolsey had the king's ear (Henry VIII, that is).

Wolsey whispered secrets into the king's ear, dark secrets from the bottom of his deep, dark well. Wolsey was the king's chief adviser, Cardinal Thomas Wolsey, the king's bigwig monster.

'Veni vidi vici. Amo, amas, amat, amamus, amatis, amant': the sound of Latin words swam through the king's ears, down through his nose and throat (they are all connected, and if they're blocked then you're in trouble. 'Ears Nose and Throat,' Mum says, and the queues go on *all afternoon*). Latin words swam up through the king's blood, towards his lungs. Wolsey had the king's heart too, at least until Anne Boleyn came along. That is just how history works.

'Wolsey, Wolsey, Wolsey.' My aunt loved Cardinal Wolsey so much I sometimes thought he lived with us. Well, she loved and she hated him, but quite where we would put him,

I don't know. There was no spare bunk bed for Cardinal Wolsey and his ego.

We heard a lot about Cardinal Wolsey's ego. Egos take up a lot of space. Egos are balloons with air pumps.

Cardinal Wolsey wouldn't fit beneath my bed, because Maze slept on the bottom bunk and the bunk beds upstairs were full now with cousins. Wolsey would have to sleep in the cellar, and he wouldn't like that much; Wolsey thought himself fit for a king. Wolsey believed he *was* the king, especially when it came to queens.

'Wolsey overstepped the mark. He went as far as he could on his ego and then he exploded, like a turkey in the oven. Pop, pop, pop, bang!'

Cardinal Wolsey's ego ran everywhere; it was like the tide creeping up over the sea wall. His ego didn't know when to stop, and before long it was spilling over the green and into the Beach Hotel, and everyone in the hotel was forced to evacuate to the beach. Soon the lifeguard would come along and tell us that to be properly safe from Cardinal Wolsey and his ego, we should set sail for France.

My aunt grinned. She liked the idea of Cardinal Wolsey exploding, Cardinal Wolsey making a horrible mess all over the kitchen floor, Cardinal Wolsey drowned in fat, Cardinal Wolsey with his tall purple hat crushed and sticky, being mopped up on the end of a broom.

'Overweening pride … the man had overweening pride. It was bound to explode. You can't keep up that kind of caper day in day out. Bang! Pop goes the weasel!'

But Cardinal Wolsey wasn't a weasel. He was a swollen hippopotamus wading his way through the siltiest mud he could find, until one day he fell into a deep bank he hadn't suspected and he couldn't get out. This was his *downfall*. Downfalls happened a lot in politics. Before long, someone was bound to head for a downfall. Plip, plop, belly-flop, and they were stuck head-down in the mud.

Politicians were always heading for downfalls. Michael Heseltine was always heading for one, and so was Alan Clark. Served them right, too. Heseltine and Clark were both handsome men, but they liked to go out on the razzle. *Heseltine was vain*, my aunt screeched, looking pleased. He was a handsome man with large eyebrows who fancied himself as an eagle. At any moment he might take off. Whooosh!

Heseltine, Clark, Healey, Heath, Howe. I remember these names from the sound of my aunt's voice yelling them out from the back room. 'Heseltine, Clark, Healey, Heath, Howe.' They were the names of politicians that sounded like the names of rivers. Politicians rolled from her tongue like water. Politicians: that was her favourite game. She loved to say their names, as though she knew them; as though she had just met them last night at a party and they'd all become friends; as though she had sat in a bar on the Thames across from Westminster and talked about the *devious* Heseltine and the *arrogant* Clark and the *dull as ditchwater* Geoffrey Howe. But he knew his stuff, my aunt said. Geoffrey Howe knew what he was talking about. *He just isn't a flashy man. He has a quiet ego. A certain kind of modesty.*

And then there was Scargill. When my aunt pronounced 'Scargill' her lip curled. She hated Arthur Scargill, she hated what he stood for, the trade unions, which meant *workers' rights*: the right to have tea breaks and sick pay, the right to go on holiday to Butlins, the right to have a lie-in on Sunday morning.

But I think my aunt hated Arthur Scargill mainly because he was scruffy. 'Scruffy Scargill ... Scruffy, Soggy Socialist Scargill.' Arthur Scargill was a soggy socialist. You could dip him in tea and he'd disintegrate. Arthur Scargill was a Rich Tea biscuit floating in a pale brown sea.

Arthur Scargill, Michael Heseltine, Geoffrey Howe, Alan Clark and Margaret Thatcher, they all lived under my aunt's bed. Stalin, the Kremlin, Khrushchev, Gorbachev, Bolsheviks, *perestroika*, the tsar, serfs, *glasnost*, words with hard, steely edges, words that cut through my brain, words announced like murder: *Stalin, the Kremlin, the Bolsheviks, the Tsar, St Petersburg, Catherine the Great (who was a great queen)* and *Perestroika. Perestroika* was the final stab in the chest and the heart. *Perestroika* was the final death blow. *Perestroika, Perestroika, Perestroika* and you were dead, laid on the carpet and caked in blood like Mrs Robinson upstairs.

17

MARGARET THATCHER
MOVES IN

After the night at the Beach Hotel, Mum began to dress differently. Her face changed. She frowned more. Mum began putting on her Margaret Thatcher look. I came home from school and there she was, the woman with the pale face, blonde hair and lipstick; the lady standing in the hall with a string of pearls around her neck; the tall lady dressed in a puffy cream blouse with a big floppy bow; the lady with a wave of blonde hair curling upwards; the woman with a shiny patent black handbag with gold clips that bit your fingers if you tried to open it; the lady wearing peach lipstick, the colour of fruit.

Everywhere I looked I saw Margaret Thatcher. She was everywhere we were and sometimes, I think, everywhere we weren't too. When we weren't looking, she was in the cellar, tidying things up and sorting out the bulbs; Margaret Thatcher was separating tulips from daffs, bluebells from hyacinths, marigolds from Michaelmas daisies. Sometimes I could hear her down there talking to herself, sounding cross.

'For goodness' sake, who on earth put all of this here? You can't possibly find anything in here … And those bikes are a death trap, an absolute death trap … I need to get to my bulbs.'

Her handbag was everywhere too. I remember it as black and gold. 'Smart,' said Maze. 'Very smart.'

Gold clasps sat on top, like a crown. I touched them and they snapped. Mum's bag was a speaking crown.

Most days I found it at the bottom of the stairs when I came in from school. Then it was at the end of the hallway when I went to the bathroom; it was under the kitchen table when I went down to pick up my knife and spoon; it was on top of the sink when I went to wash my hands. Margaret Thatcher's handbag was all over the house.

Her hair was everywhere too: whenever I looked in the mirror there was a hard turret of it; her hair was lying in the sinkhole when I drained our bath water; it was caught on the hairbrush left in the bathroom; it was flying off the front doormat when I walked in from school; it was stuck between the clips of Mum's handbag as she sipped her coffee and ate her thin white crust in the morning. Every Saturday morning I pulled out strands of hair from the mouth of the Hoover and realised that Margaret Thatcher's hair looked just like ours.

Before long, Margaret Thatcher was following us around the house. She was snapping at us to finish our homework and go outside; she was lifting her heavy bunch of keys from her black, gold-clipped handbag and yelling, 'Which one of you swines has swiped my mints?' She was frowning her face into hard lines and making her thin lips. But when she went out to the bank or the shopping arcade she was smiling her full, rich, fruity smile because she knew everyone would be looking, because everyone looked at Margaret Thatcher wherever she went, especially the people from the newspapers. 'Snap, snap, snap. Flash!'

When she went out she wore her pearls, pearls clipped at the back of her neck; when she went out, she lifted her hair high up off her face and layered it with lacquer. Then L'Oréal hairspray wafted through the house like a chemical cloud, and when we smelt the lacquer, we knew that Margaret Thatcher was about to appear. At any minute, Margaret Thatcher would be coming out of Mum's bedroom with her hair held high and tight as the pyramids. And the smell of L'Oréal hairspray would follow her all the way to the bank.

'I keep a can inside my handbag just in case the wind has a go at me,' she said. 'The wind through the arcade can be vicious, *vicious*, you never know when it might take a turn at you.'

'Best not to be caught out,' said my aunt. 'Don't forget to ask for a bit more this time. Mr Fortescue knows we keep our word. We always keep our word. We borrow but we give back. And try to find out who he voted for … it would be nice to know he was *on our side*.'

―――――――――

I remember those years with Margaret Thatcher mainly through the newspaper, those grey headlines rubbing off on my fingers as I picked it up from the front doormat. And the paper, so it seemed, was full of people shouting; there was always someone wanting to get rid of someone else over money or marriage.

One day it was J.R. Ewing from *Dallas* who was about to get it.

'Get it in the neck, J.R., get it in the neck!'

'Shhh, you lot. It's starting. Shh! For goodness' sake, sit still!'

Mum was sitting on the sofa behind us pretending not to care. But she cared very much. Everyone cared about J.R. Ewing, even Sue Ellen.

'He's got charisma,' said my aunt. 'It's in his smile, Ange …'

'Shh! It's about to start!'

My aunt pulled the curtains across to block out the light and we sat and hugged our knees and waited. Then, all of a sudden, J.R. Ewing was walking across the screen towards us, looking for Sue Ellen.

'Sue Ellen, I know you're in there,' said J.R., standing outside the shiny bathroom door.

[Bang, crash, wallop, thud. Sue Ellen falls to the floor.]

'Leave me alone, J.R. Stop your spying on me.

[A glass crashes to the floor.]

'Where is my son, you Goddamn son of a bitch? *Where is my son?*'

'You know you can't see your son, Sue Ellen. You're a drunk. Little Bobby needs a responsible mother, someone he can rely upon.'

'My son needs me, J.R. A son needs his mother.'

'You're not capable of raising a son, Sue Ellen. Bobby is gonna stay with me. You need to prove you're a responsible mother, Sue Ellen, and I don't see any of that happening anytime soon.'

[The door opens, and Sue Ellen emerges with hair stuck to her face; her eyes are large and smeared in black rings. She's been crying.]

'Now what kinda mother would appear looking like that in front of her son? You should be ashamed of yourself, Sue Ellen. Bobby isn't gonna want a mamma who looks like that. He wants a beautiful mamma, a mamma he can be proud of. You need to get yourself cleaned up, Sue Ellen. You need to make yourself look like a pretty little mamma again.'

[The scene shifts. J.R. Ewing is sitting at his desk at Ewing Oil. It's night and the lights are low. Suddenly, J.R. hears a noise. He's frightened.]

'Who's there? Bobby, is that you? Sue Ellen? Whoever it is, come out! I want to see you. Stop hiding away like a coward in the corner.'

J.R. has a whiskey in his hand. Sue Ellen would be glad to find him like this, looking like a drunk, like her. The scene shifts again. We see Sue Ellen coming up in the lift. She's inside Ewing Oil. She's heading for his office.

Sue Ellen has a gun with her, tucked inside her handbag. No one knows she's there, outside the door that says 'J.R. Ewing' in gold letters. Her doctor was expecting her, but she's taken a detour, pulled into the underground car park and taken the lift. She slips along the dim corridor clutching her bag. The office door is ajar. Casual, she thinks. How typical of him, so casual. She sneaks in.

The man she hates is bent over his desk, scribbling. She could shoot from here, she thinks. He wouldn't see her. No. She wants him to see her. She wants him to look right at her and be afraid. Not yet. She must go further into the room. She wants him to look her right in the eyes as he begs for mercy.

'Who's there?' The man at the desk lifts his head. He's looking at her. She has his full attention.

'It's me, J.R. I've come for a little farewell drink. What've you got on offer? Oh, I see you've already helped yourself. Mind if I join you?'

Sue Ellen walks over to the drinks cabinet, gun raised above her head. She helps herself to a whiskey. Then, she walks towards J.R., pointing the gun, and raises her glass to his.

'Chink, chink,' she says. 'To your health … to a good life ahead of you, J.R.!'

'Now Sue Ellen, what are you doing here? You've no business being here. I'll have to call Dr Barber and put you back in that sanatorium. We can't have you going around waving guns at people in the dark. Have you been drinking?'

'I haven't had a drink for two weeks, J.R. I wanted to keep myself nice and clean for seeing you.'

'Well, here we are. You've seen me now. Now just give me that gun and I'll take you home.'

'That's kind of you, J.R., but I'm not ready to go home yet. I've got some important business … something I've been meaning to clear up for a while.'

'You're not talking a great deal of sense, Sue Ellen. I think you need to go home now. I can run you home. Just give me a minute.'

'I don't need to go home, J.R. I've got some important business to attend to.'

And then suddenly, out of nowhere, three shots were fired and J.R. fell to the ground where he lay completely still, and everyone everywhere gasped out loud, so loud that all the televisions in England and Scotland moved an inch or two and Mum said under her breath, 'Well, you can understand why! He took away her child! He took away her *only* child. That man *should* have been shot. He *should* have got it in the neck, several times over!'

18

THE ESTATE

Dillmouth was a charming and old-fashioned little seaside town.

(Sleeping Murder)

Soon after J.R. was shot Awful Fred died. But I need to explain who Fred is, because you haven't heard about him until now. Fred was my grandfather, although I had never met him, and Fred was Awful because he married my sweet grandmother, Edna May, and made her do the washing up and cook the dinner for years.

We never saw Fred alive, so it was difficult to imagine him dead, but I tried to anyway. I imagined Fred lying out flat in the funeral home and my mother and aunt and my Aunt Jayne staring down at him and then one of them – not Aunt Jayne – would spit on his face because that is what people do when they hate someone. They spit on their face and then cover them in dust.

I do know this: nobody went to Fred's funeral except my mum and aunt and Aunt Jayne, and when they came back all they talked about was Fred's Estate. This was the story they told, the only story I know to this day.

Fred had died leaving behind two terraced cottages in Lancing on Sea. Terraced cottages in Lancing were worth thousands of pounds.

'Forty thousand each ... eighty thousand a pair,' my aunt said.

£40,000? I couldn't imagine that much money. I couldn't even imagine £1,000. What did £40,000 look like? How much space did you need for that much money? Could you sew it into your front-room curtains?

With £40,000 you'd be able to buy new curtains, a new front room, a whole new house, a large garden. With £40,000 you could buy your way from New Zealand to England and back again; with £40,000 times two (£80,000) you could buy a house in England *and* a house in New Zealand and perhaps even a house along the way. But I knew that when the money came in, Mum would start with the curtains.

> For curtains, Gwenda had chosen old fashioned chintz of
> pale egg-shell blue with prim urns of roses and yellow birds
> on them.
>
> (*Sleeping Murder*)

As she steps onto the quay at Plymouth harbour, Gwenda Reed is also thinking of new curtains. Mrs Gwenda Reed, newly married and just over from New Zealand on the boat, who, like most New Zealanders, thinks of England as Home.

But before she starts to hunt down a house for herself and her new husband, Gwenda decides she needs a proper rest first. House-hunting is an exhausting business. She will go to a hotel, a nice, steady, old-fashioned place with a comfy bed that doesn't creak when she rolls over. And the next morning she will hire a car and start her drive through southern England, across the undulating downs, towards those picturesque seaside towns she remembers from the picture books Nanny Wren used to show her between bath and bedtime.

―――――――

My mother was twenty-five when she got her first car, a grey Morris Minor she used to drive us to and from school. That car lasted a few years, just as long as Mum could drag it through its MOT, with the help of the nice man at the garage.

On cold wintry mornings her car was her saving grace. 'Better than any man,' she said, as she clawed away at the windscreen with her ice scraper. 'It'll start in a minute. It just needs some time. You can't rush it. Sally, pass me that shimmy cloth in the glovebox, and for goodness' sake do your coat up properly!'

Scratch, scratch, scratch. I can hear the scraper going back and forth across the windscreen. I look up and I see Mum's face huffing and puffing. I hear the sputt, sputt, sputt of the car as it tries to throw off the frost. Everything is frozen and still except Mum's face and hands and moving back and forth back and forth across the screen in front of me. I hold my breath in and then let it out, and I watch the cloud of white smoke disappear through the window.

When I think of Mum's car I see myself in my navy-blue coat with gold buttons running down the front. I must be seven or eight and I'm wearing a matching navy-blue hat; a piece of elastic is pinching me underneath my chin and I'm standing next to the shiny grey snail shell looking worried. This is one of the mornings when the car won't start.

'Do up your buttons,' Mum says. 'Right up to the top! It's freezing this morning. Freezing. Get those buttons closed!'

I look down at my navy-blue coat and start to wrestle with the buttons. But my fingers are stuck on the gold rim of the first one.

'Do up your lovely navy coat!' Mum loved the word 'navy'. Navy was proper and posh. If you wore navy you were smart.

I wore my navy coat to school and Mum drove me there in her grey Morris Minor. That was her car for years, until the nice man at the garage could no longer fix it and she had to hand it over. Losing her car was losing her chance of escape, because I knew that the real reason Mum kept a car was because one day she was planning to drive across the downs to London to check herself into a smart hotel. There she would put on the shimmery pink cocktail dress and sit in lovely leather chairs like the ones in Bertram's Hotel, *rich and velvet and plushy*.

There, in front of an open fire, she would find Gwenda Reed and Miss Marple sat in plush leather chairs, with a brass coal scuttle 'filled to the top with lovely large lumps', Mum said. 'To keep a warm glow,' said Miss Marple. 'Such comfy, high-backed chairs,' said Mum. 'So good on the spine,' said Miss Marple. 'Dr Quimper *would* approve.' And Miss Marple would lean gently over and tell Mum about the young woman from New Zealand she had just met who was looking for a house by the sea.

———————

Mum's Morris Minor is grey on the outside and dark pink on the inside. Cherry, Mum said, cherry leather. I asked her once how much it had cost and she told me £250, which was twice as much as our grocery bill. Starting up the car was always a bit touch and go. We were never sure if we would hear the sound of those tired sparks catching. 'It just won't catch,' Mum said. Sputt sputt sputt, said the engine. We held our breath and Mum pulled hard on the choke. Sputt, sputt, sputt.

'Not enough anti-freeze,' said Mum. 'Blast! It needs a top-up.'

Mum got out and opened up the boot. She pulled out a bottle of bright pink fluid and then went round to the front and pushed open the bonnet. Her head disappeared inside and I heard a few screechy sounds; then the bonnet slammed down and before long she was back inside staring hard at the dashboard.

'Give it a moment, just give it a moment,' she said, as though I were about to drive off with her car. The key turned.

Sputt, sputt, sputt. Grey clouds puffed up from beneath the grey mound and Mum's face tweaked slightly into a smile.

'Give it a moment. Give it a moment …' and then suddenly she turned and pulled hard on the steering wheel while she waved through the window at my grandmother who was standing anxiously on the front steps, waiting to see. As she pulled away, my mother waved like the queen at Mrs Sturgess who had poked her head out of her downstairs window to see what all the fuss was about. Mrs Sturgess usually appeared when something was going wrong. But this time she appeared just as it was turning right.

———————

Gwenda Reed hadn't thought once about the condition of the car she drove that morning into Dillmouth. She had no need. Her husband Giles had provided for her, and in any case, she had her inheritance. Gwenda was a lady after all. She was a woman of means. Gwenda could afford to spend a night or two in a hotel. She could check herself in with a pleasant smile and climb the carpeted stairs with the smooth oak banister, and run a hot bath in her private bathroom, and lie back and think of her smooth English lawn as she watched her toes gather foam.

The first thing I shall do is plant roses, Gwenda thought, the deep pink ones, closer to purple than pink, the ones with the heady scent Nanny Wren said made her feel faint. Why did Nanny Wren always make such a terrible fuss over the things everyone else loved?

'Your mother loved those roses, Gwennie dear. Queen Matildas, they're called. They quite turn my head. Makes me want to have a lie down. Now come away.'

Dear Nanny Wren. And with that, Gwenda hauled herself out of the bath, wrapped herself in the soft grey gown lying on the bathroom chair and padded off to her downy bed. Oh, I'm so glad to be here, she thought, as her lids began to drop, and now I will find a lovely little house and Giles will be thrilled and we shall live happily ever after.

And so the following morning, without any ado, Gwenda Reed drove along the south coast towards Dillmouth and her pretty little villa by the sea.

'We'll put an advert in *The Lady*, Ange. That's the place to do it. "Victorian terraced cottages nestled within sea-view".'

'Is "within" right there, Dice? You don't want to make it sound as though the view is smothering the cottages, or blocking out the light.'

'How about, "Pair of Victorian terraced cottages in clear range of the sea"?'

'Oh no, Dice! That's far too *Out of Africa*. They'll imagine elephants stampeding through the back garden!'

'"A lovely pair of terraced cottages, dating 1880s, with a generous view of the sea"?'

'Let's put the exact date, Dice. 1885. It sounds much more solid. You don't want to sound vague. People pick up on vague.'

'"A spacious pair" – give them more rather than less – "of terraced cottages built 1885 with a generous view of the sea. Suitable for newlyweds, businessmen and retired gentlefolk". No, not gentlefolk, "professionals". "Retired professionals". We don't want a horde of incontinent old men pouring down to Lancing, Ange, looking for their bottoms to be wiped. Retired teachers and army officers, perhaps the occasional newlywed couple. We have to keep those in mind. There are plenty of those about. Now, Ange, did you pick up the photos from Boots? I think we should use the ones with the wisteria. I know you're keen on the roses, but wisteria gives a better camouflage effect. Oh, and we should certainly say *Lancing on Sea*. It's worth paying for the extra letters to add the sea.'

19

A FEW FACTS

(A SHORT CHAPTER)

It's time for a few facts. Every story needs a few of those if you're going to make it work. But this is a short chapter. In fact, it's barely a chapter at all, because facts, Mum says, are usually a bit thin on the ground.

Mum was born in 1947, and my aunt in 1945. They were born and raised during Agatha Christie's heyday, the years when she was turning out bestsellers. A *Murder is Announced* was published in 1950; *4.50 from Paddington* in 1957, the year Mum was crossing Sompting green, clutching her sister's hand. *The Body in the Library* came out in 1942, the year London was being bombed, three years before my aunt was born. *The Murder at the Vicarage* was published in 1930, about the time my grandmother was out dancing with Cyril.

The Murder at the Vicarage was my first taste of Agatha Christie, and it arrived soon after my eighth birthday. I remember the opening sentence of that book better than I can remember whether we had chocolate cake or Victoria sponge, or whether *that* was the birthday the cat licked off all the pink icing, which sent Mum into an apoplectic fit, as pink as the icing, said Maze. Because it is difficult to know when it all started, this murder mystery business.

It is difficult to know quite where to begin this story, but I have fixed my choice on a certain Wednesday at luncheon at the Vicarage. The conversation, though in the main irrelevant to the matter in hand, yet contained one or two suggestive incidents which influenced later developments.

That's the first paragraph of Agatha Christie I ever read. I read and reread those sentences, and hoped and prayed that one day I would be invited for luncheon with Leonard and Greta. That soon I would find myself at lunch at the vicarage and Mary the maid would come barging in with her bowl full of greens, Mary who announces murder, Mary, which is my middle name. That summer, the summer of my eighth birthday, I fell in love with Greta and her head stuffed full of suspicions; Greta who spends her time gossiping in the grocer's and greengrocer's; Greta who loves to go to the Copper Kettle; Greta who is as open as a book; Greta who would take me out to tea and pay for everything, even if I asked for two pieces of cake.

But Greta comes with a vicar; eventually she'd have to go home, because Greta's main role is to be the vicar's wife, although she isn't very good at that. Poor Greta, you can't really blame her for being such a terrible wife; the vicar spends most of his time writing sermons. He never notices her: not when she buys a new hat or parts her hair differently or tries out a new lipstick. 'Leonard, look!' But Leonard never looks. His mind's on other things. God mostly.

Still, you shouldn't feel too sorry for them, because the vicar and his wife have Help. Her name is Mary, although Mary isn't very good at helping. Sometimes the village women find Greta with her hands stuck to the top of her head when they troop in for tea. 'Oh me, oh my! Oh me, oh my!' says poor Greta. 'How will I ever manage?'

One of these ladies is Miss Marple. Miss Marple lives in a pretty thatched cottage in the middle of St Mary Mead. Her cottage stands opposite the church. If she looked hard, Miss Marple could spy Mary from her front-parlour window; and she might. She just might. Miss Marple knows all about Mary and her wilful ways.

'She's not what I call a *sensible* girl, my dear,' Miss Marple says to Greta over tea. Miss Marple would *never* have recommended Mary to Greta if Greta had asked her opinion. Miss Marple has an opinion on everyone and her opinion is usually right. Miss Marple's opinion on Mary is that she likes to tell stories. Mary prefers fantasy to fact. With Mary, it's bound to be half-made-up.

20

WEDGWOOD IN
THE FRONT ROOM

Seeing is believing, and the truth be told, we never saw the rose-covered cottages in Lancing on Sea, as we never saw Fred's body, as we never saw Fred. Everything remained mysterious, hidden behind wallpaper and curtains. 'You should never go on hearsay,' said Maze. But hearsay was all there ever was. Money was hearsay too.

This is because no one in our house went out to work. Maze went out to work once, but that was before my aunt arrived; she rode her bike to the Zachary Merton in gale-force winds to wipe down babies' bottoms. Then once upon a time Mum worked as a seamstress, and then once upon another time she drew maps for the British government. Mum was a spy. British government agents followed her home from work, back to Sompting village, Lancing on Sea. Mum had to hold her handbag under her arm in case the agents snatched it from her, just to check she wasn't carrying anything personal on her that might give her away to the Russians.

That's when she started carrying around Fisherman's Friends. 'They'd put anyone off,' Maze said. Even spies.

Aunt Jayne had a job, but she lived in London, and we only saw her in the holidays when she came down with a purse stuffed full of £10 notes. I don't remember ever seeing money except with Aunt Jayne. The only other money I can recall are the three £20 notes plus a few coins sitting on the post office counter when Maze went to collect her pension. The money sat there for a split second before Maze scooped it up and tucked it inside her leather wallet. Then she pulled out an elastic band and tied the whole thing up. As soon as she got home she handed it to my aunt.

Money comes about when people die. And then sometimes people kill for money. J.R. Ewing was shot for money, and whoever came to Little Paddocks that night and flashed a gun around, they did it for money too.

'Money,' says Miss Marple to poor Dora Bunner, 'can do a lot to ease one's path in life.'

'Money!' Dora exclaims with bitterness. 'I don't believe, you know, that until one has really experienced it, one can know what money, or rather the lack of it, *means*.'

Miss Marple nodded her white head sympathetically. Miss Bunner went on rapidly, working herself up, her face becoming more and more flushed. 'It's the *rent* – always the *rent* – that's got to be paid – otherwise you're out in the street. And in these days it leaves so little over. One's old-age pension doesn't go far – indeed it doesn't.'

Dora Bunner is bitter about money because she's suffered. 'Gone without', Maze would say. 'If you've gone without you never forget. Pinch and save, pinch and save.'

I don't think my mum or aunt were bitter. Cross, perhaps, but not bitter. They were more like Letitia Blacklock, who always knew how to get on in the world because they had *character*, Dora Bunner tells Miss Marple. People with character got on; people without character sink to the bottom. My mum and aunt had sunk to the bottom, but they did it with character.

———————

Money was rarely mentioned in our house, but sometime after David died a social worker came round and began to ask questions. One morning a lady in brown appeared in the downstairs kitchen with a notepad and pencil.

'You've had a difficult time. Perhaps you might need a bit of help?'

'Ange is coping very well. The thing about Ange is … still waters run deep. She just gets on with it. She's been like that since she was a child. She's a natural with children. They all love her. They think she's Mary Poppins.'

The lady in brown wrote something down. 'Mary Poppins', I thought.

'How does your older son get to school?' asked Mrs Brown. She had her notepad on her knee and although she was pretending not to write, she was, in pencil, so we couldn't see.

'Angela takes him in the car. We always try to run a car.'

'That must cost quite a bit,' says the grey trousers.

'Ange has a very loyal mechanic chap. They all love her at the garage. They think her car is ever so quaint.'

'Those old cars are quite a drain, aren't they?'

'We get the royal treatment.'

'I see. And who does the cooking for you all? You're a big family now, aren't you? How many are you now? Six? Seven?'

'Seven with Maisie.'

'Maisie, that's your mother?'

'Maisie has a good little job along the sea front. It keeps her fit. She goes on her bike. She likes to be active. They all love her there.'

'So you manage on your mother's salary?'

'Yes, and Ange bakes.'

'You bake?' she said, turning to Mum.

'Flapjacks.'

'For a local ice-cream man. He has a soft spot for Ange. But the after-school children love them.'

'How much do you sell them for?'

'Ten pence, isn't it Ange?'

'Yes,' said Mum. 'Ten pence.'

'Ten pence,' said the trousers. 'That isn't a lot.'

'Enough to buy milk. We're thinking of making Rice Krispie cakes too, aren't we, Ange?'

'Yes.'

'And you claim child benefit for all your children? Five, isn't it? Four?'

'Oh yes, yes, four.'

———————

Now I think of it, I don't know how on earth we paid our rent. I suspect it was never paid. The landlord (called Frank, who was a swine, my aunt said) didn't get his rent because everything in our house was broken or ruined. Doors and windows didn't close and the front-room carpet was threadbare.

Fred's Estate would change that. With Fred's money, our house would be turned into a palace and Mum could stop covering up the front-room carpet with her old oak table.

'Well, he was so stingy while he was alive we might as well turn what he's left into something *beneficial*,' yelped my aunt. 'At least now he's dead he can do some good. Ange, what sort of ornaments do you think we should go for with the front room?'

'Wedgwood, Dice. I'd like some nice blue Wedgwood. Wedgwood will lift the place, Dice. That lovely powder blue … baby blue … baby blue and white.'

So Mum went shopping to Arundel; she went to the antique shops on the hill and brought back baby-blue and white china, the colour of strong cotton and clouds. Mum drove to Arundel and parked her car by the castle; she came back with a boot full of blue-and-white china covered in cherubs.

'My cherubs,' she said, 'my cherubs,' and stroked the outlines of their noses and faces. 'My sleeping cherubs.'

Soon a train of Wedgwood china was marching along our marble mantelpiece, and when I came home from school I found ladies in white dresses dancing along the seashore,

ladies dressed in petticoats with their legs peeking out from
fluffy skirts. 'Shepherdesses,' Mum said, 'pretty shepherdesses,'
and when I looked up I saw a large gold mirror glowering
down on them like a hot sun.

'French baroque,' said Mum. 'Seventeenth-century
baroque. I picked it up from the little shop in Lyminster.'
Mum was always going to the little shop in Lyminster when
she wasn't going to Arundel.

'A bit gaudy,' said my aunt. 'But that's the French for you.
They're a flashy lot!'

A few days later, a pink sofa arrived.

'It isn't a sofa,' Mum said. 'You ignoramuses – it's a
chaise-longue.'

'Chez-Long.' I tried to translate it. 'Chez' – with you, at
yours, staying at yours … for a long time? If you sit on the
chaise-longue I will be staying with you for a long time. Is that
what it means? A chaise-longue wasn't a sofa because you
could lie down on it and fall asleep and before you knew it
you were dreaming.

The chaise-longue was a long chair you lay down on. Aunt
Reed had probably spent several hours, maybe days, on a
chaise-longue, drifting in and out of discontented sleep. But
Jane Eyre would never have been allowed to lie down on a
chaise-longue. No. Only Aunt Reed could while away the
hours on a long pink chair with her head tipped back and a
handkerchief dipped in smelling salts plumped up on her
forehead.

Our chaise-longue was raspberry-pink.

'No it's not!' said Mum. 'It's rose, rose-pink. Deep rose, damask rose.' I looked at the chaise-longue and saw a long pink tongue curling down towards two wooden feet. The chaise-longue looked like a pink lion ready to pounce and roar.

Behind the rose-pink chaise-longue hung thick blue curtains that kept everything very still. The blue curtains hung heavy as armour.

'Rose pink and baby blue,' said Mum. 'The perfect combination. The Palace of Versailles is full of pink and blue … pink, blue and white … dreamy.'

'Versailles is very Disney,' said my aunt. 'Disney borrowed from Louis the Fourteenth. All that pink and white and blue, candyfloss colours … childish decadence. He took it all from France!' Mum nodded, as she always did, and stroked the blue velvet curtains. 'Disney dreams … baby-blue dreams, Dice, baby blue.'

21

LEARNING TO
SPEAK NICELY

A month had passed and Gwenda had moved into
Hillside. Giles's aunt's furniture had come out of store and
was arranged round the house. It was good quality
old-fashioned stuff … there was a rosewood bureau and a
mahogany sofa table. The large Chesterfield sofa was
placed near the windows.

(Sleeping Murder)

Then one afternoon I opened the front-room door and found
a large chandelier hanging from the ceiling. Sharp crystal
daggers were dangling down above Mum's favourite folding
oak table. When the door banged behind me the crystal pyramid shook and trembled. Who, I wondered, could sit beneath
that crystal monster and not shake?

But somebody did. A few weeks later a tiny woman called
Mrs Rutherford arrived to teach us 'elocution'. El-o-cu-tion,
Mum told us, was learning how to speak nicely, like Margaret
Thatcher and the queen. Elocution was holding your mouth
wide open so you didn't crush your vowels.

Elocution came from Mrs Rutherford. Mrs Rutherford was a tiny bird from Pagham Bay who came on Monday afternoons to teach us how to round our vowels.

'How Now Brown Cow,' 'Amo, Amas, Amat, Amamus, Amatis, Amant,' 'Shirley Shields Was Very Shirty Especially Early On Sunday Mornings Since She Liked to Sleep In But Her Mother Sheila Said That Only Slothful Girls Slept In On Sundays.'

'Shirley was shirty because she was dirty – and she knew it.'

'No, dear. That isn't right. We're managing the "s"s today. "Shirley Shields was very shirty especially early on Sunday mornings since she liked to sleep in and slumber."'

Mrs Rutherford made me stand in the middle of the front room beneath the chandelier to practise my 's's. Whenever I spoke, I had to address the ceiling and imagine that Queen Victoria or Queen Elizabeth was about to greet me at the door. Queen Victoria and Queen Elizabeth were on the doorstep clasping their bags.

'Raise your chin, dear. Look up towards the cornices … to the left, then to the right … Slowly, turn your head slowly. Imagine there's a large crowd in front of you and they are all dying to hear you. You are the queen of England, about to descend from your royal steed. Victoria used to ride out with her favourite manservant, John Brown. Sidesaddle of course, always sidesaddle. Ladies always ride sidesaddle, with their skirts all tucked to one side. Now let's do our Shakespeare. Fling your arms wide!'

According to Mrs Rutherford, everything had to be done with feeling. Shakespeare was only for people with big feelings. If you didn't have feeling then you didn't deserve Shakespeare.

'With feeling, dear, with feeling. From the diaphragm, dear, nice and slow. Feel the breath moving up from the centre of you. Push down on your diaphragm … Here, dear. Here.'

Suddenly the lady with the tiny face and tall hair was beside me. Mrs Rutherford was pushing her fingers and thumbs into my stomach and ribs. Push, prod, prod.

'Let the air out, release yourself from here, like a balloon, like a lovely pink balloon – slowly.' Push, prod, prod.

Mrs Rutherford's favourite Shakespeare was *Twelfth Night*. It was because of Mrs Rutherford that I started to love Shakespeare; it's because of Mrs Rutherford that I began to learn him off by heart.

The first thing you need to know about Shakespeare is that you have to speak him. You speak Shakespeare with passion and feeling. And people with passion and feeling have to hold themselves very still.

'Still as statues. Hold yourself perfectly still, dear. Now close your eyes. I want you to imagine a beautiful stone statue in front of you. Shoulders back, dear!' Mrs Rutherford pushes my shoulders back until they start to twinge.

Mrs Rutherford explained the story of *Twelfth Night*. '*Twelfth Night* is a play about bodies washed up on the shores of Illyria, dead bodies ... bodies turned into monuments. So if you're going to speak *Twelfth Night* you need to learn how to pause and be still as a statue in a graveyard, my dear.'

Mrs Rutherford looked at me hard. 'Are you listening, dear? Shoulders back ... and a deep breath from the diaphragm. Now, I'm going to tell you the story. So, stand nice and still in the middle of the room and push your shoulders back and tilt your head slightly to the ceiling ... Now, not too far up ... Gosh, that chandelier is rather large, isn't it? But let's not worry about that. Now close your eyes. I want you to imagine that image of the monument Viola speaks of.

'"She sat like Patience on a monument, smiling at grief."

'Now, who is she grieving *for*, dear? This is the question. Is it for her brother she believes drowned at sea, or another, secret love? Mrs Rutherford paused for a moment, then opened her small round mouth and continued.

'Sebastian died at sea and Viola is grieving silently for him. She's grieving for someone else too, but that's a separate issue, and rather mysterious at this point in the play. Let's focus on that secret love. Things are in rather a muddle at the moment because Viola is making a case for the love women have for men dressed as boys. It isn't the most obvious way to make your case. Now, hold yourself perfectly still, dear. I don't want to see even a flicker! Take a few deep breaths and begin ... one, two, three ... Look up!'

I looked towards the ceiling and imagined myself in Illyria. Illyria was built of sharp pointy glass. Illyria was an island of glass and light and twinkles. Illyria was a silvery place with four corners, where shepherdesses dressed in pale-blue smocks lived. Illyria was an island full of cherubs. Its shores were made of marble.

I took a deep breath and began.

'I left no ring with her. What means this lady?' Pause. I look around me. Mrs Rutherford is sipping her tea and nodding at me, looking pleased. I carry on.

'Fortune forbid my outside hath not charmed her …' Dramatic pause. Mrs Rutherford calls this *a pregnant pause*, a pause big enough to have a baby in, nine months of pause and then quite a few more after for putting your feet up.

'Not too long, dear. Just enough to let the audience feel the change of weather. You're trying to suggest *the internal life*. This is a pause for reflection. Shakespeare likes us to climb inside the mind. But we mustn't linger too long. It isn't polite.'

'Fortune forbid my outside hath not charmed her,
She made good view of me, indeed so much,
That sure methought my eyes had lost her tongue.
For she did speak in starts, distractedly.'

I pause and look left and then right to the cornices. Mrs Rutherford is dipping her biscuit in her tea. She never offers me one.

Mrs Rutherford lifts her teacup towards her nose and dips it in. 'I want to hear those "d"s, dear. "Dis-tractedly". The "d" is nearly a "t" there. "Dis-trac-ted-ly". Up on the "trac". Raise your voice up on the "t". Do it again! Up, up and away, and then tilt on the "c" before you land on the "t-ed-", then a little more open on the "ly" – the lovely soft sound of "lee" – we call that a feminine ending, dear. Lots of nice long vowel sounds at the end there.'

'Fortune forbid my outside hath not charmed her … for she did speak … in starts … distractedly.'

'Not too squeaky at the end, dear. You're not a mouse. No squeaking. Breathe deeply, from the diaphragm. Then release slo-w-ly.'

I jump some lines.

'Fortune forbid I am the man!'

Dramatic pause. I think about being mistaken for a man. I'm wearing braces. I push my hands further into my pockets. But I don't have any pockets. I start to slouch. Mum says that all men slouch unless they're told not to. It's genetic.

'Neck long, dear, like a lovely giraffe.'

'If it be so, as 'tis, poor lady …' I look up wistfully to the ceiling again. Illyria is full of clouds.

'You're not Minnie Mouse, dear. Bring down the tone. Less squeak please.'

'… she were better love a dream.'

'Shoo, Minnie, shoo! Remember, your breath controls your feelings. Don't let your breath run away with you. Unfurl slowly, like a gentle kite.'

Mrs Rutherford is looking up towards the ceiling. She's looking for her kite, but the kite is flying off to Illyria and the chandelier is tossing and turning. Soon it will fall and land on our heads.

'Fortune forbid my outside hath not charmed her! For she did speak …' I frown and then frown again. I look at Mrs Rutherford to make sure she can see me frowning. My face feels like crumpled paper. I touch my forehead. I can feel the lines.

'Not so much frowning, dear. No one has died. A woman is simply in love with the wrong man. It's quite commonplace.'

'She made good view of me … indeed so much that methought her eyes had lost her tongue …' Long pause. I look 'heavenward'. I feel my eyes starting to roll. I begin to feel dizzy, and tip over.

'Nice and straight, dear. Lift up your shoulders and draw deep from your diaphragm. Remember, your diaphragm is your well. Draw deeply from it. Draw deeply from your well. Lift yourself up out of the well. Leap like a frog, up towards the air!'

'For she did speak …' I start to grin. I can feel the smile move across my face. 'She loves me, sure!' I grin.

'Good, that's right, a nice little explosion of joy, joy at the thought that someone might love you, just for that moment. At that sure moment you forget all the muddle and misunderstanding this might bring.'

'The cunning of her passion invites me in this churlish messenger …' I try to curl my lip. I think of the three musketeers and their moustaches. I twirl my moustache and I point my beard. 'None of my lord's ring!' I shake my head. I shake it again and again.

'Not too much, dear, you don't want to make yourself seasick.'

'Why, he sent her none.' I pull up my head and stick my nose in the air.

'Not too movie-star, dear. Try to control yourself. Small gestures, small things. Discretion. Acting is the art of discreet moves.'

'Poor lady, she were better love a dream.' Whispy. Mum listening to Sinatra, or Sinatra singing to Mum.

'No, no, no, dear. Not too movie-star. This is *Shakespeare*.'

My favourite part was coming up. 'Disguise, I see thou art a wickedness.' Cross. Margaret Thatcher thinking of Arthur Scargill in his tatty anorak. 'Wherein the pregnant enemy does much. How easy is it for the proper-false in women's waxen hearts to set their forms!'

A candle melting, slowly, sadly, making a big mess all over the kitchen floor. Women's hearts are melting candles. They don't last for long.

'Snuff it out quickly … Go on!' says Maze.

'Alas, our frailty is the cause, not we, for such as we are made of, such we be.'

Jane Eyre speaking to Mr Rochester. Someone with a bonnet on. Mrs Tiggy-Winkle.

'How will this fadge?' Like fudge. Dig your teeth deep down into it. Eat it. Eat whatever comes. 'My master loves her dearly; and I, poor monster, fond as much on him.' Getting quite hysterical now. Mr Rochester when he finds out Jane won't stay at Thornfield. Mr Rochester running around the parapets with no scarf on. 'And she, mistaken, (silly idiot) seems to dote on me.' Very hysterical now. Mrs Tiggy-Winkle when her cakes have burnt. Mr Rochester thorough bush thorough brier.

'What will become of this?' Shrug my shoulders and throw my hands in the air. Look as though you've just lost everything. Mum after the council have bulldozed through her roses. Mum *after all this*.

22

THE MAJOR AND HIS WIFE

At Christmas, Mrs Rutherford brought my brother and me a box of Thorntons toffee. Thorntons toffee was brown sticky square pavement slabs packed away inside a box. I peeled open the waxy paper and stuffed one of the squares into my mouth.

'Now dear, one more poem, I think, before I go. Let's have Tennyson, "The Lady of Shalott". Let's hear those nice lapping sounds.'

But I was still squelching through delicious toffee rocks and mud in my mouth and I couldn't speak. So Mrs Rutherford left me, mouth stuck and speechless.

'Greedy guts,' said Mum. 'You should've waited until the lesson was over instead of stuffing your face. How rude! What will she think of us?'

She slammed the front-room door and the chandelier shook. I sighed and looked at the clock above the mantel-piece. In ten minutes Mrs Stapley would be here asking for her nice cup of tea and scone, Mrs Stapley who was married to a colonel. Or was it a major? 'A retired high-ranking officer,' said my grandmother. 'Very grand. You'll have to be on your best behaviour. Mind you don't slurp your tea.'

Major Stapley and his wife lived on the edge of Lobs Wood on the corner of Maltravers Drive. Maltravers Drive was a wide leafy road with a curve in the middle. Mum loved Maltravers Drive, mostly because of its curves.

'Curves bring mystery, Sally. Nobody wants to walk in straight lines. We can leave that to the Americans! Everyone loves a bit of curve, it feels more like a country lane.' Mum went all dreamy. 'Maltravers Drive is such a pretty road. I hope they don't ruin it by pulling down all the trees.'

All the houses on Maltravers Drive stood back from the road. They had driveways filled with crunchy gravel that let everyone know that you were coming.

'Did you drop the note off, Sally? There was a cheque inside. I hope you put it through the door properly and didn't leave it in the porch.'

When Mrs Stapley came to our house she never rang the doorbell. She always rapped on the window, which made you jump. I think she did that on purpose. She told me once that she used to do this when she was teaching at the Gels' School to make sure they were awake during their lessons. Rat-a-tat-tat-tat on the window.

'You have to be firm with young gels, otherwise they take advantage of you. Young gels are clever. They aren't all like you, dear.' She paused and looked at me for a moment, then carried on.

'Of course I teach maths now for fun. At the Gels' School they all did very well. Mathematics then was pure, good and hard. Mathematics was difficult. Proper fractions, not these babyish things they ask for now … These scones are lovely! Are they home-made? No? Well never mind. My daughter always makes lovely fluffy fresh scones, fresh and fluffy as a baker's hat. Now, we can eat our scones and think about fractions. You should never stop thinking about mathematics. See this scone, for example. I'll cut it in two, or half; and then I cut that two into another two, and we have four parts, or quarters. And then again … This is getting a bit tricky, isn't it dear? Can't your mother make slightly *larger* scones?'

Mrs Stapley looked down at the crumbly mess on her plate and shook her head. 'Oh dear. Well, we'll have to manage with what we have. Cut those four parts into halves again and you have … Well, you have a bit of a mess really, but if the scone were *larger* … It doesn't take much to make them larger, you know. You should tell your mother just to make a little more room on the baking tray. The whole point of a scone is to pile up as much jam and cream as possible. At the Gels' School we had a cream tea every Friday afternoon after hockey. Cook made them nice and fat and fluffy, like a duck's bottom.'

Mrs Stapley spent most of her time cutting up scones. She sat beneath the dangling chandelier, which she occasionally addressed with a butter knife, and cut up scones. Each scone was cut into four parts and carefully covered with butter. Each part was then safely tucked away inside her mouth. A long pause followed between each mouthful. But she always came back to the same point: how many spoonfuls of jam were needed to cover two scones, and how many knifeloads of butter.

'Now, I think you should only have a fraction of what I have – two to one, don't you think? What is two to one of four, Sally?'

A lot more for you, I thought, and a lot more crumbs on your side of the table. Longer for you to eat, less time for doing maths. But I don't mind. I hate maths.

———————

Major Stapley came once a week, on Thursday, to teach me Shakespeare and English history. Mum always made a big fuss around the major arriving.

'The major is here, Sally. Hurry up. Sit up nicely. Don't slouch, and remember to hold your shoulders back and breathe deeply. Don't mumble! The major told me he didn't think you were engaging very well last time. You *really* must concentrate. There's no excuse for not being able to learn a few lines off by heart. We had to learn *heaps* of Shakespeare when I was at school – whole scenes. For goodness' sake, make an effort! None of this is free, you know!'

But the major's Shakespeare was for boys, not girls, and Mum didn't understand that I wanted to learn more of Viola's speeches, or Titania's, Queen of the Fairies. *Twelfth Night* was set by the sea and *A Midsummer Night's Dream* was full of flowers and fairies. I liked Viola's slow, melancholy speeches. I liked the sound of Puck warning of the arrival of Oberon:

The King doth keep his revels here to-night;

Take heed the Queen come not within his sight;

For Oberon is passing fell and wrath …

But the major only wanted me to read *Henry V*. Henry, he told me, was England, and Henry was *magnificent*!

I dreaded the shuffling sound of the major on the stone steps, the rat-a-tat on the door and the beaky nose poking round the corner of the hall.

'You must stand to attention when he comes in, Sally,' Mum said. 'Make sure you stand up straight and salute him.'

Why should I? We weren't in the army. There wasn't a soldier in sight, and no amount of reciting of *Henry V* was going to bring troops marching into our front room.

But Major Stapley wanted us to fill our hearts and lungs with the sound of English kings charging over the top of English hills; the cries of English soldiers facing down the French. He wanted to make soldiers of us, but I kept saluting the wrong way.

'Brutes. The French are absolute brutes. Crude souls and turncoats,' the major barked.

I didn't know how you knew whether someone had a crude soul or not, unless you cut them open. How did you even begin to find someone's soul?

'Right! Let's begin! Take a deep breath and look out towards your troops. Timing is everything in battle, as it is in Shakespeare. Iambic pentameter should sound like walking or marching. Confront those lines aggressively. You are about to face your enemy. Quick march ... and charge!'

I stood with my feet squirming on the carpet and began to tremble. The words wouldn't come. I couldn't move. The French were going to get away with murder at this rate. 'Once more unto the breach, dear friends, once more. Once more unto the breach, dear ones, once more, once more, once more.'

'Start again, and count your "once more"s. One at the beginning and one at the end. Imagine you are marching through marshy fields and meadows, one-two-three, one-two-three, swinging your arms and beaming with the joy of your homeland. Remember, you are a young king prepared to give your life for your country, a young king who knows he is also God-on-earth. "Once more unto the breach, dear friends, once more!" Ka-ta! Now stride forth with your arm raised and imagine you are plunging a sword into the breast of a French brute, a French beast. Ka-ta, Ka-ta Ka-ta-ta-ta!' the major barked as he rose unsteadily to his feet and plunged an imaginary sword through my school skirt.

'Now lift your sword ... feel the valour of the moment, the valour of your mission! You are here to save England from those French varmints! Graaah!'

I lifted my sword high, but all that came out was, 'Once more, once more, once more ... unto the breach, dear ones.' I sounded more like Mrs Tiggy-Winkle handing out treats than Henry V lunging down a breach.

'Take some deep breaths and pull up tall ... Imagine you are God-on-earth and this is your moment of heroism. All of

England is watching you. You are about to make history! Murder the buggers! Do your worst! Trample them into the ground!'

———————————

I never saw past the front door of the house on Maltravers Drive, but I imagined that the major and his wife were just like Colonel Easterbrook and his wife in *A Murder is Announced*, sitting at breakfast reading the papers.

'Archie,' said Mrs Easterbrook to her husband, 'listen to this.' Colonel Easterbrook paid no attention. He was busy reading *The Times*.

'Archie, do listen. *A murder is announced and will take place on Friday, October 29th, at Little Paddocks at 6.30 p.m. Friends please accept this, the only intimation.*' She paused. Colonel Easterbrook smiled at her affectionately.

'It's the Murder Game,' he said. 'That's all. One person's the murderer, but nobody knows who. The lights go out. The murderer chooses the person he's going to murder. It's a good game – if the person knows something about police work.'

'Someone like you, Archie. You had to deal with all those interesting cases in India. Why didn't Miss Blacklock ask you to help organise the game?'

It was true that Major Stapley had spent time in India, where once upon a time he had ridden elephants and met begums and baboos. That was before he met Mrs Stapley, who stopped him doing all of that. Mrs Stapley was working in a school in India teaching all the 'dear little things in dhotis how to do their sums. But there wasn't much point because the poor little mites had nothing to count, except grains of rice,' she told me wearily as she sipped her tea and scoffed her scone.

'India was the jewel in her crown,' my aunt said loudly. 'The Indians know how to run railways. They learnt it from the British, of course, but they know how to run a decent train service, better than we do.'

But then the major retired from India and came back to live in a small seaside town. Mrs Stapley came back with him – she'd had enough of the small brown bodies dressed in dhotis who couldn't do their sums – and began working in a Gels' School. Mrs Stapley – who was called Margaret – decided that she didn't mind marrying a man ten or fifteen years older than she was, an old man who walked with a stick, if it meant she got a nice big house by the sea with mullion windows and wisteria around the walls. No, she didn't mind one bit, she told her sister Agatha, if it meant she could order fresh fish for supper three times a week and home-made scones from the local bakery. She could even afford to hire a gel.

Mum had found the major and his wife through the local paper. She placed an advertisement in the *Arun Gazette* and one day they answered the advert. It was the lovely creamy writing paper that persuaded Mum. 'Look, Dice – properly embossed.' That and the fact he was a major, of course.

Since Fred's Estate, Mum had spent hours looking through the personal ads column for old furniture. But people advertise in the *Gazette* when they want jobs done too: Handymen, Gardeners, Maids, Detectives and Tutors.

'Private Tutor wanted to teach teens to speak Shakespeare nicely. Must like tea and scones. An Army man preferred. Will take wife.'

23

THE BODY IN THE LIBRARY

In between speaking Shakespeare, I was still reading Agatha Christie. I couldn't give her up, not yet. I read and reread her, and then I found her short stories. So I read and reread those until I knew them off by heart.

Because when I grew up I was going to write detective stories. I would write about people who live together for years and years in the same village, sometimes in the same house, and then one day, for some reason, usually involving money or missing relatives or both, they decide to organise a cruel party. Their chief guest is Murder.

You read detective fiction because you want to be frightened. You read it because you want your flesh to crawl with ants; you want to feel the goosebumps rising. I reread *A Pocket Full of Rye* to frighten myself. I was terrified at the thought of poor Gladys, the maid found in the garden of Yewtree Lodge. I minded about Gladys Martin. I minded as much as Miss Marple did.

Miss Marple minded because she had trained Gladys to be a maid from an orphanage and Gladys had left and gone off to work in cafés because she had liked boys and wanted to be seen by them. But boys never took any notice of Gladys Martin because she wasn't pretty. Gladys was spotty and plain. She wore bad clothes, or rather the clothes she wore never suited her because, truth be told, Gladys was quite fat.

'Life is cruel,' says Miss Marple, 'I'm afraid. One doesn't really know what to do with the Gladyses. They enjoy going to the pictures and all that, but they're always thinking of impossible things that can't possibly happen to them.'

Poor Gladys Martin, who everyone calls adenoidal because she speaks through her nose rather than her mouth. Mum hated it when we did this. She hated it so much she sometimes covered my brother's mouth with sticking plaster. But it was my aunt who put her up to it, because in the end it was always my aunt.

How undignified! Miss Marple says it is 'an affront to human dignity … such a cruel, contemptuous gesture'.

Gladys Martin haunted me, Gladys Martin with her squashed-pegged nose. I already knew the name Gladys because my grandmother had a sister called Gladys who was dead. I knew nothing about Gladys except that she had been silly. Gladys had been a giggly girl; Gladys liked to giggle. Gladys couldn't help giggling.

She was always behind her hand, Maze said, full of giggles. But girls are like that. Maze must have told me that, or perhaps it was my aunt who told me that *Maisie* was silly and Maisie made me think of Gladys. Gladys and Maisie have blurred. My aunt didn't think much of either, not even though Maisie was her mother. 'Candyfloss between their ears … not a real thought in their head … such silly girls, always giggling.'

———————

Everything I know about Gladys comes from what Maisie knew. And now I think about it, Maze must have known more than my aunt, because she had her photograph, the one she carried in her purse, always inside her purse in the middle pocket. And Maze grew up with Gladys, who was before my aunt – before, not after.

The only picture I can hold in my head is from that photograph, the one of Maze and Gladys sitting on the pebbly beach. Maze says it's Shoreham beach with a lighthouse, but you can't see the lighthouse in the picture. They cut it out, whoever took the photograph. When I think of Gladys on the beach I see a girl with a big grin giggling into the back of her hand at the slightest thing. I imagine her eating sandwiches when no one was looking, Gladys with her hand in the picnic basket nibbling on the cheese and chutney sandwiches.

Gladys Turner was my great-aunt. I wonder if she was what Inspector Neele in *A Pocket Full of Rye* calls 'the adenoidal type', the sort who wouldn't say boo to a goose. Inspector Neele recognises Gladys Martin's type when she comes into the interview room to be questioned. He knows that Gladys is frightened to death; he must be patient:

The girl who entered the room with obvious unwillingness was an unattractive, frightened looking girl, who managed to look faintly sluttish in spite of being tall and smartly dressed in a claret coloured uniform. She said at once, fixing imploring eyes upon him, 'I didn't do anything. I didn't really. I don't know anything about it.'

Gladys Martin is a frightened little child; she is a stunted child. She is a baby still. At thirteen, I was no Gladys Martin. I knew not to speak through my nose, and I wouldn't have been frightened of talking to inspectors.

———————

All crime writers have to learn to write a good plot, and most plots are like playing a board game. Murder is playing a game that goes right or wrong, depending on what side you are on; and murder can be as easy as winning a game of tiddlywinks. Tick, tick, tack and you're gone in a second, swallowed inside that small plastic hole. Murder is a game of tiddlywinks, and at some point most people imagine murdering someone, even if it's just for a second.

Take Aunt Reed. She'd love to strangle Jane Eyre with her bare hands, and Jane Eyre would love a turn at boxing her aunt's ears. Once she started she wouldn't be able to stop. *Temper, temper, temper* says Aunt Reed. That's what does it. Temper is what leaves you with blood on your hands. Temper is what gets you thrown into the Red Room. Everyone has a Red Room somewhere inside them, with blood on their hands.

Murder is the stuff of dreams, except with murder, those bad dreams turn into something real. Then Bertha Mason really does come into your room while you're sleeping and tear up your linen veil. Rip, rip, rip, gnash, gnash. Claw!

And then there is the silly sort of dream, pure fantasy, but with just a smack of reality to make it absolutely delicious. That is silly Dolly Bantry in *The Body in the Library*.

***

One early morning in June, Dolly Bantry, wife of Colonel Bantry, is enjoying a lovely dream. In her dream, things are going very well: she's just learned she's won first prize at the flower show for her sweet peas. Dolly can see the vicar holding a splendid silver cup with her name on it. Dolly is beaming.

Just behind the vicar, she can see her old friend Miss Jane Marple looking a little bit miffed; and behind Miss Marple, she catches a glimpse of Mrs Price-Ridley looking very miffed indeed. Dolly is pleased to see this, and she beams some more.

She turns to look at her cup and sees her flushed face reflected in it. Above her head, small white clouds float by. Dolly looks up towards the blue and white sky and to her delight finds her name scrawled in the clouds. Her smile grows larger and larger. I'm grinning like the Cheshire cat, she thinks to herself in her dream.

But suddenly her dream is interrupted by the sound of squawking outside the door. How rude, Dolly thinks. I was having such a lovely time. She sighs and turns over, but she can't block it out. There is more noise.

The squawking is followed by a clatter of teacups and a loud scream. The silver cup and the smiling vicar vanish and

Dolly is forced to open her eyes. She sees that the curtains are still drawn.

Downstairs, doors are banging and Dolly can hear the sound of sobbing. What a hullabaloo! What a nuisance! She turns to her husband and gives him a jab. 'Arthur! Arthur! Wake up. Something's going on downstairs. I can hear all sorts of banging and screaming. Go and find out what on earth it is.'

'Eh? What did you say?' There is a heavy groan from the space beside her.

'Go and see what's going on, Arthur. There's a terrible commotion. Something must have happened.'

'Good God, woman! It's Sunday morning. Leave me to my sleep, can't you?'

'Arthur! Please will you go and see what the noise is all about. There might be an intruder or something. He may have a weapon!'

There is a loud groan and a shake of the blankets.

'Oh, God, Dolly! All right!'

The colonel hauls himself from his warm bedclothes and begins fishing around for his slippers on the floor. He trudges towards the door and pulls hard on the handle. The door clicks open.

He can hear voices rising up the stairs. Joseph, the butler, is standing at the bottom looking pale.

'Good morning, Colonel. Bad news, I'm afraid. We've found a body in the library.'

'What? A body? Are you sure, man?'

'Quite sure, Colonel, I'm afraid. I think you should come and see for yourself.'

———————————

Early one morning my brother Peter and I found a body in our front room. It was the body of a man we'd never seen before, and when we caught sight of him sprawled out across the pink chaise-longue we screamed.

Mum came running. 'What on earth is all this racket?' She looked pale.

'There's a man asleep on the sofa. Look!'

'For goodness' sake! That's David.'

'Who is David? David who?'

'Di's friend. He's an old friend from the past. He's come to visit. You do remember him, you've just forgotten.' Mum looked around and sniffed. 'It was a long time ago. I don't suppose he'll be staying for long.'

Mum looked down at the man, whose hair was sticking straight up into the air. She looked cross, as if she wanted to put him out with the rubbish. 'He's offered to do a few jobs around the house. He might as well be useful while he's here.'

But how on earth did he get here? I looked down at the man slouched on the chaise-longue and thought that he must be an alcoholic. Men lay about like that when they had done something bad, usually a lot of drinking.

Mum said the man was David, as though we should know him. But David was from the past, and the past was too far away for us to see. I peered at the man with thin brown hair, the man who was thin all over, the man who looked like a twig snapped off a tree. Someone might scoop him up and put him out in the garden with the leaves and the worms.

'Garden rubbish … it'll make for some nice garden rubbish.'

Garden rubbish was orange peel and apple cores and soggy cabbage leaves and old bits of dried bread. Garden rubbish was good for the roses. But garden rubbish takes years to break down, Maze says.

Bodies decompose too; that's why you have to bury them quickly. Colonel Bantry knows that the minute he sees the young woman with platinum-blonde hair lying sprawled out on his expensive oriental rug, the one he'd brought back from India. Colonel Bantry knows that when you find a body, you have to get it out, quick-smart. Bloody entrails seep into carpets and leave a terrible mess.

I looked down at our new velvety carpet covered with swirl-ing blue and cream shapes and I saw figures moving around, two thin people holding hands, two people roaming round and round the garden like a teddy bear.

Two thin people are walking around in circles, chanting words and praying. Two people with brown hair are up against the garden wall where Mum grew her roses. I can see the roses bobbing in the background. On the other side is the apple tree where we threw our buckets up into the branches. But there are no buckets in the tree and no children, only two thin people with their eyes closed pressed up against a wall with the tree hanging down over them. David and Sue, Sue and David. *Sue and David up a tree, k-i-s-s-i-n-g.*

David was married to Sue. Or Sue was his girlfriend. I didn't know which. It didn't matter. But once upon a time, David had been with Sue and they were walking around our garden holding hands. David and Sue looked as though they might be going to church. David and Sue were in love. Then something happened, but we didn't know what, and now Sue is gone. She had never been seen again. Not since that day in the garden. Now there is only David lying slumped on the pink chaise-longue in the front room.

Once upon a time, Sue had been a name pinned to a tree. But her name had blown away. Or else someone had torn it off. And now, no one was sure what Sue's real name was. Was it Blunt or Barnes or Baxter or Black or Blackie? Was it Bird? Sue was a little bird shot from the sky; a tiny blackbird that tumbled from the tower.

24

BERTHA

I've always been afraid of Bertha Mason, the dark-haired woman who belongs to Mr Rochester. Bertha is the past and the past is bad, and so Bertha must be kept upstairs, out of harm's way.

In her attic room, Bertha crawls around like a wild cat. She hisses and bites at the window; she scratches the paint off the walls with her nails; she clings to the curtains with her teeth. Poor Bertha Mason, no one would recognise her now.

'The state she's in. Look at her hair, all matted and messed up … just like a witch! Poor Berthy, Berthy calm down, calm down. We're here to help. Here, help me pick her up, Rog. She needs a good washing down. Help me with her legs … Blimey, what dead weights they are! What've they been feeding her on? Can you get her ankle, David? This is a three-man job. We might need to call the others in … we need more hands on deck. Cor, did you get a whiff of that? I don't think this lady's had a bath for weeks. Tie her feet together, Rog, she's kicking like a mule. She needs to go back upstairs!'

But Bertha wasn't always like this. Once upon a time she had another life, filled with sunshine and fresh air. Once,

Bertha Mason giggled and tossed back her hair. She wore white cotton dresses with lacy hems that showed off her strong brown legs. She laughed and smiled at men.

Bertha Mason grew up in the Bahamas with a brother called James. Once upon a time they played hide-and-seek among the palm trees and ferns.

'There you are, there you are,' her brother said. 'I can see your pink dress, Berthy, and your toes are peeking out! And Berthy, I can hear you sneeze! You shouldn't hide among the flowers, silly goose, they make you sneeze! Go further back into the dark trees. Go back into the dark, Berthy, where the bark is rough and the nettles sting and the ivy covers your body in green tangles!'

In the Bahamas, Bertha Mason hid among the trees and counted to twenty. Then there was only her brother to come and find her. 'There you are, Berthy, among the dark trees. I can still see your dress, you silly girl. Cover yourself up with ivy!'

The Bahamas are in the Caribbean. Pampas grass and coconut trees grow there. Every day is blue and green and yellow. The Bahamas are full of bright light. Once upon a time the queen of England ruled the Bahamas. She took holidays there. The queen liked the Bahamas, so she decided to stay:

Dear Charles, I'm having a lovely time here in the
Bahamas. The locals are very friendly, although they could

do with covering up a bit more. Yesterday a lovely gel brought me the most delicious banana cake with my morning tea. I think I shall stay on another day or two. Be sure to water the cacti, dear – but not too much, they only need a drop or two.

Soon after I was born the queen gave the Bahamas back to the Bahamians. The Bahamians were quite relieved; they liked the queen well enough, but the people of the Bahamas wanted to be in charge. Who could blame them? This was what James told me, anyway, James, who was my first best friend, James, whose dad shipped bananas from the Bahamas.

———————

James and I spent all our time together and when we were six we decided to get married. We sat in the concrete tubes all through playtime and discussed our future.

James told me this: in the Bahamas they lived in bungalows, small white roofs surrounded by palm trees. I would go back to the Bahamas with James and live with him in his big white house. We'd plant plantains and palm trees; we'd build a plantation. At the end of the day we'd sit on our terrace and look out to sea. James would bring me tea with milk and on Sundays I'd get out a tall ladder and polish and wax the trees. Then a breeze would lift my hair and my legs and arms would turn brown and when I sat next to James no one would think I was white as the milk we drank in our tea.

———————

Later, when I read *Jane Eyre*, I thought of Bertha Mason and my friend James: if only James had married poor Bertha everything would have been all right! Bertha would have stayed in the Bahamas; she would never have come to England. Bertha would never have been sad and mad. Mr Rochester shouldn't have taken her away from the sun and the sand. They say it's cruel to move cats.

But Bertha was taken to a big stone house full of rain and clouds. Bertha married a man who took her back to England; a man who told her that the sun shone at least once a week, and always at the weekend. But it didn't, and Bertha missed the sun badly. After a while her hair fell out and she lay in bed all day and cried.

Bertha began to turn wild. She longed for the sun and the soft breeze on her face; she longed for a glimpse of the sea. So Bertha pulled up the sash windows and climbed out of the stone house filled with clouds. She crawled along the window ledges and up over the roof. Bertha sat on top of the turrets and wailed for her banana trees and blue sea and palm trees. She lifted her hand to the sky and sighed. 'Oo-leee-ooo-leee-laa-aaaaaa. Ooooo-eeee-waaaa-waaaaa, waaaa-waaa-waaa.'

Bertha gnashed her teeth and turned her head to the sky, but the God of the Sun and the Stars, the God of the Wind and the Rain was nowhere to be found.

———————

When I first read *Jane Eyre*, I couldn't sleep for months thinking of Bertha. I saw her everywhere. She was there when I closed my eyes and began to drift off to sleep. Bertha was there, crawling along my bedroom ceiling; she was sliding down the wall on her thick long hair; she was hanging upside down and turning somersaults. And when she turned towards me I saw her big gummy mouth and white teeth and they were dripping.

But some nights I saw another face: she was thin and pale and her hair was shorn and when I looked into her eyes they were scared. Her hair was so thin I could see the pink skin on the scalp beneath, and when she turned her face towards me I saw nothing but a big black hole. In my sleep I watched her climb down off my bed and crawl towards the corner of my room. I watched as she began to lick herself, the small woman with thin brown fur, the woman with tiny brown wings.

Something creaked: it was a door ajar; and that door was Mr. Rochester's, and the smoke rushed in a cloud from thence … in an instant, I was within the chamber. Tongues of flame darted round the bed: the curtains were on fire. In the midst of blaze and vapour, Mr. Rochester lay stretched motionless, in deep sleep.

(*Jane Eyre*)

In another century, in a different world, Bertha Mason would have been sent to hospital for trying to set Mr Rochester's bed alight. She would have been put on a side ward and kept under observation. Every fifteen minutes a nurse would come in and check her pulse, lift up her eyelids and make a note on the whites of her eyes. Twice a day Bertha Mason would have been given a dose of clozapine to keep her meek and mild and lying in bed in her white cotton gown.

Instead, Edward Rochester keeps her in the attic above his bed under lock and key. There, he hopes, she will be quiet and timid as a mouse. Under lock and key.

But Bertha Mason can't be quieted and at night she begins to moan and roam. At night she starts to laugh, and once she starts, she just can't stop. She laughs and laughs and laughs. She roars.

It is her laugh that wakes Jane. Then it is Jane who roams down the long dark hallway, and up the stairs, up to another dark corridor, to another set of stairs, and then another and another. Jane keeps climbing until she reaches the top.

At the foot of the highest stairs she freezes; the moaning sound is so close she can practically feel it on the back of her hand. It is coming from under the door; it is hot and sweaty, this moaning, the hot breath of a woman panting flames.

Jane stands and shivers. Then she lifts her hand and reaches for the white door. But before she can reach the handle something hot touches her foot. A tunnel of flames chases her down the hall.

PART THREE

25

ON HER SMALL
BROWN WINGS

'Take her away to the Red Room, and lock her in there,' says
Aunt Reed after Jane boxes her ears. 'The mood of the revolted
slave was still bracing me with its vigour,' says Jane. 'Four
hands were immediately laid upon me, and I was borne
upstairs.'

'No jail was ever more secure,' says Jane to herself as she
begins to look around her. She spies a white chair that looks
like a throne. She goes over and sits in it, but the chair is icy
cold. She shrieks. A moment later she catches sight of a
mirror; the image in the mirror frightens her. Who is this
strange person, this pale phantom staring back at her?

The strange little figure there gazing at me, with a white
face and arms specking the gloom, and glittering eyes of
fear moving where all else was still, had the effect of a real
spirit: I thought it looked like one of the tiny phantoms,
half fairy, half imp.

———————

I can't quite tell you how it all came about, but at some point something strange took over: a fairy person, a phantom, a revolting slave, and I was no longer myself but someone quite different and strange.

I first noticed her when I was ill with measles and I spent all day lying around in the front room. I was tired and bored and couldn't do anything at all. But every now and then I got up to look at myself in the mirror, because the thought of measles frightened me: those red spots all over my forehead and chin. What were they doing to me? How far would they go?

Mirrors do strange things. Whatever you see in a mirror is bound to look peculiar. 'Best not to pay too much attention,' says Maze. 'They never tell the truth.' Mirrors distort and bend things out of shape. Mirrors tell lies. No matter how hard you look in a mirror you never see what is there. Not really.

In my house there were no mirrors. There was a tiny one above the bathroom sink in the downstairs bathroom, but no one lingered there to look at themselves because it was always too cold. 'Brrr!' said my brother. 'Brrrrr! It's so bleeding cold in here you could build an igloo! Give me that towel!'

'Bleeding?' said Mum, who always heard rudeness a mile off. 'There's no bleeding about it. Mind your words. Now get a move on! You should be done by now. Get that towel over you.'

After Fred's Estate, an ornate gold mirror appeared in the sliver of space outside Mum's bedroom. 'French baroque,' my aunt said with her eyebrows lifting towards the ceiling, her eyebrows flitting up and down like angry crows. 'French baroque,' she said to the mirror, as though it would speak. 'Now, I don't want any "Mirror, mirror on the wall" from any of you lot. This is a mirror for adults. It's there to create space. Mirrors bring space. They open things up. Now get off with you! You're blocking off all the light. Give the mirror some space, for Pete's sake. She's only just gone up.'

But the mirror didn't really change anything, because behind that mirror lay our dark hallway with no lightbulb and the damp kitchen filled with cardboard boxes and the bathroom growing green mould. There, behind the mirror and the boxes stacked high, Mum was reciting her favourite Dylan Thomas poem, in the early-morning bathroom, with the blue light coming up and the window open on the latch and the wind poking through to clear out the steam.

Mum said the window must always be open because otherwise the damp would creep in and take over. But the damp had already taken over. Mum just didn't notice. She was too busy saying her poem, which sounded like prayers, prayers spoken to the angels.

I stood in the dark hallway and I watched Mum's mouth opening and closing on the words that hurt her, the words that brought tears to her eyes, the words that never brought angels.

'The conversation of prayers about to be said by the child going to bed and the man on the stairs who climbs to his dying love in her high room, the one not caring to whom in his sleep he will move and the other full of tears that she will be dead, dead, dead … turns in the dark on the sound …'

But when Mum turned there was no one there. No one, no one, no one, except me, creeping down the hallway towards the bathroom door waiting for the bath and hoping that soon it would all be over. The poem, I mean.

Still, Mum kept going, right to the end, to the top of the stairs and back down again, because once you start saying a poem it is hard to stop. Your mouth just keeps moving. Or maybe it's your soul pushing you on. Anyway, Mum went round and round, up and down and up and down, pouring water over her head and shoulders and down her neck until she lay down in the water, lay down as though she were dead, washing off the soap and giving herself a good rinse, she said, rinsing herself off properly, because you didn't want to get a rash, so you had to lay dead for a while until you had got rid of the soap which might cling to your skin and never go away. Never. And then you'd be in trouble. So you lay beneath the water until you could feel yourself clean all over, clean and tingling, even if it meant you had to lie like the one who lies dead.

Mornings, very early, before the light came up, Mum sat in the bath and practised her Dylan Thomas poem about the woman in her high room and the man on the stairs and the child not caring to whom in his sleep he will move. The poem about the woman dying in the tower and the man on the stairs moving up to her like the tide coming in to cover up her dead body and wash her away. And the child who drowns as the tide washes him away, and the man standing on the stair crying and looking on and the woman in her high room sleeping, for ever and ever amen. And all without God watching, or maybe all with God watching, I couldn't tell. I could only see Mum's face as she rinsed off the tears with her favourite Pears soap which doesn't hurt your eyes, so don't be such a baby. Now hurry up and get out. The water's getting cold!

And when she had finished, Mum pulled herself out of the bath, dragged all of her white thighs and legs and arms and belly to the top of the stairs, to the high room where the woman lies sleeping. She lifted her leg over the bath edge and looked for one quick moment in the bathroom mirror and then looked away.

———————

There was only one full-length mirror in the house. It was in the small hallway outside the upstairs kitchen, and it was white with a gold rim. One day I stopped to look at myself in the mirror. I looked and I saw a silent face staring back at me.

'Mirror-gazing will lead to vanity, and vanity is a sin! Don't be such a vain creature. Get away from there!'

I jumped. Dark hair reared up behind me. Dark hair filled the mirror. Dark hair was breathing down my neck. She was speaking.

'There is no need to spend all that time admiring yourself. Now get away. Vanity is one of the seven deadly sins!'

Vanity. What did it mean? 'Vanity' – it had sharp edges, and the edges went straight into my stomach. 'Vanity, vanity,

vanity'. Vanity was a long white van you drove around full of mirrors. Before long the van crashed because the mirrors at the back distracted you. Vanity was a crushed white van with a smashed face and a bleeding body. Vanity was a broken and bleeding mirror. Vanity was a dead body with sharp glass stuck in it. Vanity was what led to the police. Vanity would get you a life sentence. Vanity would lock you away for the rest of your life in a cold and draughty attic room.

> What a consternation of soul was mine … how all my
> brain was in tumult, and all my heart in insurrection!
>
> (*Jane Eyre*)

Sometimes the things you do are a mystery, to yourself, to anyone, even to God. Sometimes people are a mystery to you, those special others you cannot quite pass as blank. Jane Eyre was a mystery to me: she was *my* mystery and she kept drawing me back. Now, years later, I know for sure – it was Jane Eyre who led me away, Jane on her small brown wings.

That winter I pushed aside the thick velvet curtains and I stepped onto the ledge. I ruffled up my brown wings; I flapped and flapped. Then I flew, up into the sky towards the dark blue sea, where the Northern Ocean, in vast whirls, boils around the naked, melancholy isles; and the Atlantic surge pours in among the stormy Hebrides. I flew to the far-off place where the spirit of Jane Eyre lives and breathes.

26

EXPERT OPINIONS

Soon after, I took myself to the doctor to ask his opinion on this pale person in the mirror. What a consternation of soul was mine! How all my brain was in tumult! Because I knew that doctors were forbidden in my family; no one in my family ever went to a doctor.

But a doctor, I decided, would at least be someone with a different opinion. Doctors are experts with expert opinions. A doctor's opinion counts for a lot, sometimes even for murder.

Emma Crackenthorpe from *4.50 from Paddington* knows this. Emma Crackenthorpe trusts doctors. She knows that a doctor is just as good as a policeman for dealing with a body. Doctors are discreet. They keep secrets. Doctors are polite and discreet and sometimes they are stimulating. Dr Quimper is interesting because of the way he crosses the hall. Dr Quimper is a stimulating visitor. He comes with something new and strange, with his expert opinion. *He was a tall genial man, with a casual off-hand, cynical manner that his patients found very stimulating.*

———

As I walked towards the surgery on Maltravers Drive, I wondered whether the doctor would be casual or intimidating and whether I could trust him. What *can* you tell a doctor, I wondered, and what can't you? How casual or stimulating should *you* be?

Maltravers Drive was intimidating. It was full of large houses set back from the road. Big driveways and tall trees hid the houses so that people passing by couldn't peer in.

'Lovely and private,' Mum said about Maltravers Drive, which was her favourite road. 'Well positioned … nicely set back, and room. And those lovely established trees. The council needs to make more of an effort to plant trees. Why should the people on Maltravers Drive be the only people who can see trees from their front room?'

The surgery was at the top of Maltravers Drive. It was a blank brick building with glass, hemmed in by trees. I went to the front reception and asked to see a doctor. A woman with a gold chain around her neck stared at me. She lifted a pencil from behind her ear and opened the large book in front of her. She leaned forward and I could see white, white bosoms. She leaned back and her mouth opened slowly and I saw white teeth flecked with bumpy red lipstick. The red lipstick was so thick it looked plastic. I wanted to poke it to make it crackle.

'Do you have an appointment?'

Of course I didn't. How could I make an appointment?

'No. I don't have an appointment, but I'd like to see a doctor. I want to ask him some questions.'

A piece of bacon flicked out from between the red plastic. The piece of bacon curled and uncurled then folded back inside.

'We don't have any free appointments until five. You'll have to wait. You need an appointment to see a doctor, you know. You can't just waltz in and expect to see someone, not on a Friday.'

The gold chain dropped sharply and made a scratchy sound on the counter. The red lipstick disappeared inside a large white book. Then a shiny nose poked up. 'You'll have to wait. Go and sit in the waiting room. The doctor will call you when he's ready.' She pointed to the room across the hallway.

The waiting room was covered in blotchy wallpaper. I wondered if it was supposed to remind you that you were ill. It was the colour of sick. If you didn't feel ill looking at that wallpaper, then you weren't really ill. That was the test. You had to be ill to go to the doctor, probably quite ill. I wasn't ill, but I needed to ask some questions.

There were magazines lying around on a table, but I didn't bother to look at any of them. They looked boring, all about women's hair and teeth and thighs and going on holiday. Instead, I thought about the doctor. I'd never met a doctor before. What were doctors like? In Agatha Christie, doctors are *professional* and *pleasant*. A dead body is *unpleasant*. Dr Quimper is unmoved by the sight of a dead body. Doctors mustn't betray emotion. You might ask a doctor's opinion, but you don't expect him to take up too much space. Doctors are discreet. They arrive suddenly and they leave quickly. They carry a brown case and they keep their diagnoses to a minimum. Doctors are like the houses on Maltravers Drive: very private.

A man dressed in a brown suit with black hair and a large forehead came out of a side door. I heard my name, 'Sally Bayley?' and I jumped. The name was a question. The man in brown was asking me a question. He was walking towards me and holding out his hand and the hand was a question too.

'Sally Bayley?' he said again.

I couldn't speak, so I nodded, and I followed the man in brown through the white door, the door he was holding open for me. I went in.

The office was still and calm and square. It was so square that I started making outlines of the room in my head, square upon square upon square. I drew squares around everything to keep me calm. Inside one square, a plastic skeleton leaned against a wall. A window was open and a small breeze lifted him slightly; he tilted towards me. His eyes were dark and hollow and his jaw hung open. I looked away and stared at the desk. Here was another square. The doctor's hands were folded slightly; they were folding and unfolding. They weren't quite square, more like pyramids, moving pyramids. I didn't want to look at his face because I knew it was beaming at me. I knew that his forehead was glistening and damp. He was hot; this room was too stuffy for him, for both of us. He should open another window and let in some air. The window: another square.

'How can I help you?'

I didn't know what to say. I had come all this way and I

didn't know what to say. I clutched at my knees. I couldn't find the words. This wasn't a room for telling stories in.

'Are you feeling unwell?' The man in brown touched his hair and wiped his brow. Perhaps he was feeling unwell.

'I wanted to ask a few questions.'

'What about?'

I hesitated. This was going to sound stupid. 'About me, I suppose. I think there's something wrong with me … At least, my aunt thinks there is. I've changed … She says I've changed … Or she means I've changed, even if she doesn't say it. I'm not how I used to be. I'm pale all the time. My mum says so too. I'm *too thin and pale*, she says. I can't tell, I don't really notice … But they make it sound like it's serious, so I thought I'd better ask a doctor. They don't like doctors at home.' I paused and looked at the man in the brown suit. 'We've never been to a doctor in my house.' I stopped.

The man in brown was frowning slightly. He looked confused. 'Well, you do look a little pale. But that's nothing to worry about. Are you eating? Do you have an appetite?'

'I don't know. I don't think I eat as much as I used to. I had measles and then I stopped eating for a while.'

I stopped and looked down at the floor. The carpet was flat and green and made up of small squares. I started to count the squares. I didn't know what else to say. Then I blurted out, 'I think I'm just very different from the rest of my family. That's the problem. We don't get each other. Sometimes, it's like living in a zoo. I'm the strange animal that doesn't belong … the thing in the corner.'

The man in brown smiled and leaned forward. 'Families are a lot of work, I know.' Then he stopped and smiled again. He liked to smile. He liked smiling more than speaking. 'Let me just have a quick check of your pulse and your heart rate. You do look pale, but plenty of people in England look pale. You wouldn't be the only pale person walking around here, would you?'

I think he wanted me to smile, but I couldn't. He opened a drawer and took out something with rubbery tubes – a stethoscope.

'Let's just see what your heart is like.'

He pressed something metal to my chest and leaned in and listened. 'A strong beat. Nothing wrong there. Let's just check your pulse.'

He lifted my wrist and pressed down two cold fingers. 'Nice and strong there, too.'

The doctor smiled again and looked at me and said, 'What I think you might need is a nice chat with our social worker, Audrey. We have a very good team here, and Audrey is marvellous. It might be a good idea for you to get some things off your chest. It sounds as if there's quite a lot going on at home.' He paused, and then rather than smiling looked quite serious. 'I do know your mother ... I knew your mother years ago. She was a very lovely woman.' He paused again, but didn't smile. 'Things were quite different then ... quite different. We all believed in something ... the eternal mystery.'

When Agatha Christie's Lucy Eyelesbarrow enters the library to tell Emma Crackenthorpe that she has found a dead body in the Long Barn, Emma Crackenthorpe wrongly assumes that she has come to discuss a domestic matter. Lucy has had enough of Rutherford Hall and all its oddities; she will be leaving imminently. *A shade of apprehension* passes over Miss Crackenthorpe's face. *In such words do useful household staff announce their departure.*

I returned from the doctor longing to announce my departure. I wanted something that could extract me from my house – a rare disease, imminent death, something more than an oddity. The doctor's idea wasn't going to make a blind bit of difference. What did a social worker do anyway? It sounded like something my aunt called a Left-Wing Thing, a half-baked idea, wishy-washy nonsense. But I worried that I might have started a Left-Wing Thing, and at any point the Left Wing might march through the door of my house and start sharing their ideas. Doctors must be full of Left-Wing ideas, ready to spill out of leather cases or from the inside of rubbery stethoscopes. Mr Crackenthorpe (who is called Josiah) thinks this; he doesn't hold his doctor in high regard. *A regular old woman inclined to wrap me up in cotton wool,* says Josiah Crackenthorpe. He means Dr Quimper. *Fuss, fuss, fuss, says Josiah. Got a bee in his bonnet about food.*

But the doctor I saw didn't have a big enough bee in his bonnet. I needed someone else to make the fuss. I should have taken someone with me, I thought. Betsey Trotwood, perhaps. She'd have pooh-poohed the idea of a social worker then bashed the man in brown firmly on the head and demanded a cottage by the sea in Kent.

Miss Marple manages this. When she goes to see Dr Haydock for a consultation, she suggests some nice bracing sea air and he agrees. London is too stimulating and St Mary Mead too damp. Dr Haydock suggests Eastbourne, but Miss Marple says it's too cold; she suggests Dillmouth, a nice, quiet little town by the sea. Dr Haydock knows she's up to something, but he goes along with it. He writes her the doctor's note that will get her sent to Dillmouth. Dr Haydock folds the note nicely in two and passes it over to the old lady he has known for years.

Miss Marple tucks the note carefully inside her handbag. She looks up and gives one of her small, barely perceptible smiles.

27

SOCIAL WORKERS
AND SOULS

Getting anything in the adult world is a matter of giving someone the right answer. Miss Marple knows this, and so does Betsey Trotwood. You present someone with a story as though it were a pressing fact, and more than likely they will swallow it.

The other way to go about it is to produce new elements, fresh opinions. This is bound to lead to conflict – people don't like strangers barging in – but if you introduce someone new into the story, they might just back you up.

Audrey Taylor was a woman with long hair and flowing shirts and flares. When I first met Audrey I was sure that she was one of the coloured people. Once upon a time Audrey lived in Babylon and she hoped and prayed for Zion. Audrey Taylor knew her way up and down the stairs and through the white door. She didn't carry castanets but I think she might have had them hidden in her handbag. Sometimes I thought I could hear them rattle.

Audrey Taylor was a medieval saint. She had a big wide forehead with a chequered handkerchief strapped across it. Sometimes she wore her hair up in a bun or in a ponytail, and then she looked like a Mother Superior. But she almost always wore trousers, wide flares that flowed from her bum like blue waterfalls. On top of her flares she wore a knitted Aran jumper that curled up around her wrists. I never understood why she liked wearing an Aran jumper but I thought perhaps she must like the irritable feeling close to her skin. Saints like to suffer.

Like most adults I knew, Audrey Taylor was religious. Audrey was religious and so was Dr Bollinger. I don't think they were supposed to speak about God, but sometimes they couldn't help themselves.

Audrey told me that she always prayed before she came to see me, which made me feel as though there must be something very wrong. People only say prayers when they are in trouble, or when other people are in trouble. Big trouble. Matters of Life and Death.

If you are religious you say prayers to save souls. It's hard to explain exactly what a soul is, but I'd say it's the biggest part of the human body. You just can't see it, because it is made of air. A soul is the air you blow inside a balloon to give it shape, and only God can blow up the balloon.

But souls can burst. Audrey and Dr Bollinger believed my soul had burst and needed mending. Somebody had made a hole when I wasn't looking. Out, out went all the air. Splat, bang, wallop. Thud. Only a lot of prayers could blow it back up again – the prayers they said behind the closed white door.

Audrey prayed with Dr Bollinger behind the surgery door, and I wasn't allowed to go in; but I don't think they were saying prayers exactly, I think they were wailing them. Perhaps when things get really bad with souls you have to wail your prayers, otherwise God just won't hear.

I'd arrive at the surgery and the lady with red teeth would tell me to go and wait in the Consulting Room.

'Now don't mess around. Sit nicely on the chair. They're in a meeting. They'll be out soon.' Glasses moved up her face and she opened her mouth and pecked her teeth. Birds. Ladies always look like birds. Birds with their mouths about to open for worms or berries, red berries, chocolate and lipstick.

In the next room Audrey and Dr Bollinger were praying and wailing. I sat next door in the perfectly still room, until they came out with those smiles on, those big, broad, wide-as-the-sky smiles, as though they'd been up to Heaven and back again and God had whispered in their ears and told them where to find my soul, among the stormy Hebrides.

My soul was lost, and the only way to get it back was to work on my feelings. Audrey and Dr Bollinger worked on feeling, and feeling is a lot of work. This is what they told me, anyway: that feeling was the thing. I had to feel my way back to my soul; and feeling was religious.

Dr Bollinger only once listened to my chest with his steth-oscope, only once took my pulse. The rest of the time it was all feelings. What they wanted most was for me to talk about feelings in front of my mum and aunt. If I could do that then my soul might be found. Audrey and Dr Bollinger believed that they could help me open some doors and windows and let in some air. What they meant was that I could let in the feel of the Holy Spirit. But the Holy Spirit takes a lot of feeling to arrive, even more than Betsey Trotwood has over her special patch of grass and the terrible donkeys; or Mum for her roses; more even than Jane Eyre in the Red Room, who's furious enough to smash a mirror.

But before the Holy Spirit could arrive the fateful letter had to be sent.

———————

It was a dark day in November when the letter arrived. It was a perfectly ordinary letter, in a perfectly ordinary envelope, but at the top of the envelope was stamped, in pink letters, 'Westcourt Medical Surgery, Child Support Services'.

Whisssh! And the small white envelope floated down through the letterbox on the breeze and lay just there, on the mat.

It lay there until my grandmother picked it up as she came in with her early-morning shopping. Without her glasses, my grandmother couldn't see the red circle with the address at the top, so she didn't know what she was pushing under my mother's door.

Letters can cause a great disturbance. Letters are hidden hurricanes sealed away in small white parcels. Once opened, they can wipe out everything around them, everything you once knew, everything that had been there right from the start.

Think of David Copperfield. He suffers from the terrible disturbance of a letter arriving one morning at the house of his aunt, Betsey Trotwood. By now, David is living with his aunt in Kent, near the white cliffs of Dover. A lot of things have happened in between, far too many things to tell. All you need to know for now is this: after David's mother dies (she's called Clara, but you won't remember that), his cruel step-father, Mr Murdstone, moves in. Not long after Betsey Trotwood flounces out, Mr Murdstone barges in with his spiteful sister, Miss Murdstone. Soon there are plans to send David away to school, but David hates school, so before that happens he runs away, and the place he runs to is his aunt's house in Kent. David runs away towards the cliffs of Dover where Betsey Trotwood lives.

At the present time, Betsey Trotwood lives downstairs from a man called Mr Dick. Mr Dick is obsessed with writing a history of Charles I (that's the king who had his head chopped off). Anyway, Mr Dick calls this his Memorial, which is the bee in his bonnet. Betsey Trotwood and Mr Dick are not married and nor is Mr Dick her boyfriend. They have a *distant connection*, says Betsey Trotwood, who is very clear about this.

Mr Dick has a backstory. His family thought him mad. According to his family, Mr Dick *went that way*. But the real trouble starts when his favourite sister *takes a husband*. This is just too much for Mr Dick, and he begins to crumble. His sister was his whole world.

Soon after the taking-of-the-husband business, Mr Dick's brother places Mr Dick in a mental asylum. His family says this is necessary because of his madness. What they really mean is that Mr Dick is a peculiar sort of chap. Maze says that when you go all peculiar you are more than likely to find yourself flat out on the hallway floor without knowing how you got there. I think Mr Dick was just too full of funny turns for his family to manage. After all, the hallway floor is a long way down.

Fortunately, Betsey Trotwood knows this and she steps in and takes Mr Dick off to live with her. As a matter of fact, Betsey Trotwood has a soft spot for Mr Dick. Why else would she scrape him up from the floor? In any case, this is how Mr Dick comes to live upstairs in the house, around and about the cliffs of Dover.

But to return to the letter.

'I have written to him,' Betsey Trotwood announces one morning at breakfast. David looks blank, then anxious, so Betsey Trotwood continues. 'To your father-in-law,' she says. 'I have sent him a letter that I'll trouble him to attend to, or he and I will fall out, I can tell him!'

David is petrified. He can't finish his breakfast. He can't drink his tea. He can't sit still. 'Stop squirming,' Mum says. 'For goodness' sake, sit still. What is it? Have you got ants in your pants?'

But David knows letters can cause disturbance. Letters carry threats and warnings. Letters bring people to you, but they also take them away. Some people believe they are messages from God. For David Copperfield, the letter that came back from Mr Murdstone was a message from the Devil, and the Devil was throwing black rocks.

'I have sent him a letter that I'll trouble him to attend to, or he and I will fall out, I can tell him!'

'Does he know where I am, aunt?' I inquired, alarmed.

'I have told him,' said my aunt, with a nod.

'Shall I – be – given up to him?'

'I don't know,' said my aunt. 'We shall see.'

28

A MOMENTOUS INTERVIEW

The anxiety I underwent, in the interval which elapsed before a reply could be received to her letter to Mr. Murdstone, was extreme; but I made an endeavour to suppress it.

(David Copperfield)

The first time she came to the house Audrey Taylor was dressed like Paddington Bear. She was wearing a duffle coat, and I thought that that might be something at least, because Mum liked duffle coats. She thought they were practical and smart.

But then, when I looked at Audrey again, I saw that she looked wrong. Audrey was wearing a duffle coat which looked too long; she looked like a piece of stretched toffee that someone had chewed on for a while, but it was too late to do anything now, because Audrey was knocking on our front door.

When Audrey knocked the house shook. She knocked on the door and I shook, from head to toe. Audrey knocked on the door and every bone in me quaked. She knocked on the door and the curtains and window frames jumped. Audrey knocked on the door and my mother and aunt's faces – the faces sat in front of me on the pink chaise-longue – turned to thunder.

———————

Thunderclouds are looming the day the Murdstones arrive. David Copperfield sits in the front parlour opposite his aunt and watches her face; her face will say everything. He only has to watch his aunt and he can tell what sort of storm might be coming. Betsey Trotwood's face is 'a little more imperious and stern than usual', but she isn't flummoxed. To be flummoxed is to wear a face that says everything. Betsey Trotwood would never look flummoxed; her mind is always on the job, and the first job in hand, when she looks out of the window that morning, is to deal with that nuisance woman riding rough-shod all over her special green patch. How dare she? The cheek!

No, that morning Betsey Trotwood is the opposite of flum-moxed; she is outraged, her face is full of fell wrath. Her sacred space, the space she jealously guards from the straying donkeys, the space where her housemaid, Janet, is sent several times a day to shoo them away – 'Janet! Donkeys!' – that space is now being trampled over by a lady with a sharp face riding sidesaddle on a donkey.

'Janet! Donkeys! Janet! Donkeys!' And Betsey Trotwood sounds the alarm.

———————

Thus I began a new life, in a new name, and with everything new about me. Now that the state of doubt was over, I felt like one in a dream. A curtain had forever fallen on my former life. No one has ever raised that curtain since.

(*David Copperfield*)

No alarm went off when Audrey Taylor walked into the front room. Only the lines on my aunt's face turned harder and her mouth clipped tight. 'I won't be trespassed upon! I won't allow it! Go away!' Betsey Trotwood was in the front room, speaking loudly from beneath her bonnet. But Audrey wouldn't have noticed this.

And she wouldn't have noticed my mother, who sank back into the chaise-longue. She wouldn't have noticed Betsey Trotwood even, with her big flouncy bonnet on, because her eyes were fixed to the floor and her hands were sat in her lap as though she were about to say her special prayer, the prayer about the child who is drowned. And my mother's eyes were closed. Her eyes are closed and her arms are outstretched and she is flying off to the one who lies dead.

And my aunt is standing, tall and imperious, in the centre of the room, like a sentinel waiting to deliver her message from God, and her mouth opens, and the black rocks start flying, they fly and fly around the room, smashing the windows and cracking the mirror and shattering the dancing shepherdesses on the mantelpiece, until one large rock hits the chandelier and the pointy pyramid crashes to the floor. It crashes on top of Audrey Taylor and her toffee-coloured coat and Audrey is buried alive among millions of tiny fragments. And Audrey screams. She screams and screams. She wails, because she has glass all over her hands and hair, she has glass in the back of her eyes, she has glass between her teeth.

When Audrey spoke my mother winced. When you wince, your skin jumps, and your teeth too. When Audrey opened her mouth Mum jumped out of her skin and she stayed there.

'I'd like to suggest a contract.' Audrey was speaking, she was speaking and smiling, her hoping-for-the-very-best smile. She was perched on one of the pale-blue chairs, chairs with wooden scrolls at the top of the arms. I sat apart from her, on the matching chair, clasping the arms and running my hands up and down the scrolls, hoping they might fold me away inside them.

Audrey was moving her mouth and speaking.

'I think it would be a really helpful idea if we all made a contract together. What do you think? Something we can all refer to. That way we can reduce some of the conflict and perhaps build bridges.'

'Build bridges?' My aunt's mouth snapped open. 'Do you know of anyone who actually built bridges successfully? Brunel … Brunel did. Is that what you mean by building bridges? You want us to be engineers? Well, we just don't have the space for that, I'm afraid!'

Audrey looked flummoxed. When you look flummoxed your eyes glaze over for a moment and you are not sure where to look. Sometimes you look down at the ground. Audrey didn't do that – she just kept on beaming – but I could tell she was flummoxed because her eyes went a little duller. They had less spark on the inside; they were running out of light.

'I mean that it might be useful if we all agreed that Sally would spend a certain number of mealtimes with you all, with her lovely big family.' Audrey was trying hard, too hard. I winced.

'Our lovely big family?' My aunt's eyes were turning into bullets. They were becoming narrower and smaller, like small slits to start with, for a bullet to fly through. The bullet would come next. The bullet always came. 'How many are there in our lovely big family? Do you know? I find it hard to keep count …'

'Let's see … Sally has told me about your lovely family …' Audrey picked up a small black notebook sitting on her lap and began leafing through the pages. 'Well, she told me …'

'Did she? What exactly did Sally tell you? She seems to have been very keen on telling you things.' The dark slits were narrowing. I could feel the bullets loading up. Soon there would be another round and we would all be lying on the floor under broken glass.

'Twelve children and three adults.' Audrey had got to the answer.

'Well, you've been doing your homework. Next you'll be telling me all our names.'

'Well … let's see …'

'There's no need for that. We know who we are, thank you. We don't need a school register. Now perhaps you could tell us exactly why you are here and what you want. I expect she's been telling tales.'

'I think Sally needs to talk.'

'Grah!' A strange growl leapt across the blue carpet and I screamed.

My mother lifted her head. 'Stop it, Sally, for goodness' sake!' Then she bent back down again. My mother was saying her prayers; she was whispering her poem about the man on the stairs.

Audrey turned towards me and gave one of her smiles. I winced. She looked back at my aunt and turned up her beam.

'I think if we can agree that Sally spends a certain number of mealtimes with you, then you will feel as though she is still part of you all. If we build a contract together then we'll feel as though we've all been heard …'

Audrey's voice trailed off. Another growl was flying towards her. Thump! It landed in her lap. It tore at her blue flares, it ripped open the bottom of her Aran sweater. But Audrey kept going. Audrey was good at that. *Just keep going, Auds, just keep going. Don't give up, girl, that's my girl.* That's what her mother must have told her. Or perhaps that's what you learn when you become a social worker, because the fact is most people won't like you, no matter how nice you are, and Audrey was very nice, but she was interfering. At least that is what most people would say. But it wasn't her fault; that was her job. She'd been sent to interfere. Poor Audrey. I felt sorry for her.

'This will help us all compromise,' she said brightly. 'This way the contract will do all the difficult work for us. If you have something written down, you can all consult it.' She looked down at her notebook and began scribbling. She seemed pleased.

My aunt's lip curled. 'A bit like negotiating an overdraft. Ange is good at that, aren't you Ange?' Mum nodded, as she always did.

'Except that all negotiations can be ignored, can't they? People agree to all sorts of thing and then sign off on them, but those bits of paper don't mean anything at all. They're utterly worthless … like so many marriages.' My aunt paused and gave one of her fake smiles, a smile that sent chills down your spine because it was so bright, and today she had on her lipstick. Even brighter.

'Are you married, Ms Taylor?'

Audrey stopped scribbling and looked up. She hadn't expected this sort of thing.

'As it happens, I am. But perhaps we could continue with the contract? We're doing rather well.' Audrey looked a little ruffled. Her wings were put out. But Audrey wouldn't fly away. Audrey always stayed to see things through. 'Come on Audrey, love. You always see things through. You're a good Christian girl, and good Christians have stamina.'

Audrey continued. 'We've agreed that Sally will spend most mealtimes with you all. She won't stay late at school. She will do what the others do, the other children I mean, but two days a week she can do her own thing.'

'You see, it's rather different if you're married. Marriage brings a certain sort of mind-set.' My aunt was ploughing right over her. Audrey blinked and held her pen tighter. Hold tight, Auds, hold tight.

'We don't share that mind-set, so you can't just waltz in here and tell us how to raise our children. We don't share the same point of view. This is a family without men. We've decided we don't need them. In fact, we're doing rather well without them. Sally is just trying it on, as all teenagers do. It's all a bid for attention. You don't need a degree in psychology or social work' – she paused and looked directly again at Audrey – 'to work *that* out.'

Audrey's forehead puckered up. She looked worried. Things were spilling over. She needed to tip the cup back up the right way. She dipped down towards her tea and raised her teacup to her mouth. She needed something to hide behind, but her spoon was clattering too loudly. Audrey's hands were trembling. Keep going Auds, keep going.

'What lovely china. So delicate. Is this a family heirloom?'

'Wedgwood. A good family. Unique. You know a Wedgwood anywhere. An old English family.'

Audrey looked pleased. She started again. She'd done this before. She could do this. She could! 'All families are unique. There's no set rule about that, obviously. It's just sometimes families need a bit of extra help.'

A strange noise came from my aunt's mouth. Not a growl, but a screech. She was trying to speak, but her mouth was freezing over. The lipstick was turning icy cold. I looked at her eyes. They were small, dark bullets. She turned them straight towards Audrey.

'Bang, bang. Bang.' The room was suddenly very dark. 'Bang, bang, bang.' My aunt shot Audrey straight through the nose and teeth. Then she went for her pale-green eyes. She shot out all her tiresome smiles, all her earnest glances, all her sympathetic downcast looks, all her bright beams of hope. I could smell gunpowder. It was the smell of rage.

'I don't think we need the sort of help you are suggesting. Ange and I have managed quite well by ourselves. We've had our little experience with Social Services. You've come round with your little notepads and pens, with your sociology degrees from your redbrick polys, and you expect us to listen to your glib little diatribes. We've had to deal with tragedy here, *real* tragedy, not just the little bit of dysfunction you might read about in a sociology textbook … a textbook no doubt written to satisfy leftie tendencies.'

My aunt paused for breath for a moment. Her eyes were tiny black pins. She was ready to fire again. 'It's all nice ideas for you lot, with your pretty ideologies and your left-wing principles and your dungarees and duffle coats …'

I watched Audrey's face. She was wincing slightly. Her feet were shifting back and forth. Her hands were turning pages over and over. She was twirling her pen. Now she was biting it.

'… and your Home Counties husbands …'

'Ms Bayley, I really think now that if we keep going …'

'No! we're not going to keep going! At least not the way you think. If you want Sally to sign up for some sort of contract that isn't worth the paper it's written on, then go ahead with that. But Ange and I are having nothing to do with your limp, leftie gestures. If Sally doesn't want to comply with our way of doing things, then perhaps it's time she left home and found somewhere else to put herself. I'm sure that you lot can find her a decent home with sugar and spice and all things nice. Isn't that what little girls are made of? Isn't that what you are made of, Ms Taylor? Sorry to be so personal, but this is a personal matter after all. Perhaps Sally could come and live with you? I expect you have a nice little place in the country …'

She paused and looked directly at me – bang – and then directly at Audrey – bang, bang, bang.

'After all, what you are really saying is that the way we do things here isn't quite to madam's sensitive needs.' She looked at me again, and this time it was hatred that was boring holes through me. Large, wide holes.

'Well, if we're not good enough for her, you're welcome to her, that's all I can say. I don't suppose she has the first idea what she's got herself into – what she's dragging us all into. Well, we're a family here, not a set of selfish individuals. A family is like a tree: when one branch gets diseased, you lop it off.'

Somewhere I heard a large gasp, but it didn't come from Audrey and it wasn't from Mum. The sound was both near and far, outside the door, beyond the front steps, over on the sea front, across the scudding waves, up in the windblown clouds. Somewhere, someone was gasping very loudly and I thought it must be God coming up for air.

29

THE INEXORABLE

But in his countenance I saw a change: that looked
desperate and brooding – that reminded me of some
wronged and fettered wild beast or bird, dangerous to
approach in his sullen woe. The caged eagle … whose
gold-ringed eyes cruelty has extinguished.

(*Jane Eyre*)

There are some things you can never recover from. Mr
Rochester knows this. When Jane Eyre wanders off into the
early-morning light, he is ruined, like the old house he lives
in. He crumbles away. When Jane Eyre returns, some years
later, she finds a desolate man.

By then, Mr Rochester has assumed a different shape.
For one thing, he's stopped wearing his hat. *I heard a
movement – that narrow front-door was unclosing, and some
shape was about to issue from the grange. It opened slowly: a
figure came out into the twilight and stood on the step; a man
without a hat: he stretched forth his hand as if to feel whether it
rained.*

Poor Mr Rochester, who is now blind. Poor Mr Rochester who now needs a guide, someone to give him a good steer.

I've never been blind but I think sometimes not seeing everything that lies ahead means you just carry on. You don't know what you're up against, so you just keep going along the path you've already fixed on, because you can't see anything else. There's no looking left or right or up or down, only carrying on.

This is what people mean when they say things are 'inevitable' or 'in-ex-*or*-able'. There is no *or* about it. Being *able* to carry on is all you can do. Nothing else. You are stuck staring at the *ex*, the way out. *Ex* is the moment you might just lose your nerve. But you don't. You place your other hand on top of the latch to stop the trembling and push up hard until you hear the click.

By then it's all over. By the time you've clicked open the latch you are already well on your way out; by then something is pushing you, some invisible spirit, some reckless sprite, something quite hard and inexorable.

———

After Audrey's visit, after the letter arrived, nothing was ever the same again. Circumstances were altered, and I saw a change, a very large change. After Audrey came, no one would look at me. Whenever they saw me coming they turned away. They had sent me to Coventry.

And I knew this: that Coventry is a nasty town in England. I asked Mr Drake at school where Coventry was and he said somewhere near the Midlands, which is the middle part of England, but he was quite vague. Coventry, he said, is a place built from concrete because Coventry was bombed badly in the war. Coventry Cathedral was bombed very badly by the Germans; Coventry had to be built again. Coventry is covered in concrete. Mum would hate Coventry. There is nothing she loathes more than grey concrete. It really gets her goat. That's why she hates the flats along the front.

'They should never have been built. It's a disgrace, an absolute disgrace.'

After the Momentous Interview, after Audrey came to visit, after the Experts Barged In, I was in disgrace. I was stuck in nasty Coventry. That winter Mum sent me to Coventry and I never really came back. Mum put on her best Margaret Thatcher face and for years she didn't take it off. I'd seen that face before. It was the face of Betsey Trotwood as she looks out from her parlour window upon the Murdstones; the face of Aunt Reed greeting Mr Brocklehurst on the drawing-room carpet; the face of Miss Marple as she greets Dr Quimper at his surgery desk; the face of Miss Blacklock ushering Inspector Craddock across the threshold of Little Paddocks.

And then one day, in the middle of Coventry, I came home from school and my aunt was wielding an axe. She was swinging an axe high above my head. That was the day the trees fell and I tumbled from the tower into the cold, dark sea.

I came home from school and she was there, glowering in the upstairs kitchen where my grandmother sat making cheese on toast looking worried, my grandmother with her face turned towards the wall. And that's when The Woman Upstairs, the woman I remember sitting on the floor in a downstairs room, cross-legged and chanting, began to yell. That woman, the woman in my dreams.

I've had quite enough of your antics. I'm sick and tired of all the trouble you are causing. How dare you drag Social Services into this, and what business do you have going to the doctor like that? You're a selfish little bitch for dragging all of us into this mess, just because you need to feel special. You're beginning to remind me of my friend Sue. Sue went that way ... She had to be taken away ... Sue was weak ... She had no backbone; that was her trouble. She wouldn't say boo to a goose but she didn't have any insight either. Sue was too meek for her own good. She hadn't grown up. Arrested development, that's what it was, a case of arrested development, anybody could see that. She went that way because she hadn't any character. Yes, Sue was weak. That was her trouble. And now, look at you, you're going that way too.

Sue, Sue, Sue, Sue, Sue. You, You, You, You, You. Fee-fi-fo-fum, I smell the blood of an English girl ... Your bones will never grow ... Osteoporosis. Bone disease, that is. Lack of calcium. Broken bones. Your bones will break ... they'll never mend. You'll grow fur! After a certain point, you'll grow fur! And then no one will want you, no one, no one, no one, and above all you won't be a woman, woman, woman. You won't be able to breeeeed. You won't grow breasts, you won't be able to feed children, and children are the mainstay, children are the source of life, children are what women are born for, to breed bairn, as your useless father would say. And where is he now? Where is he now, the drunken sod?

And then suddenly I was on the floor; I was rolling around on the carpet. I hit the carpet and I rolled, I rolled and I rolled, down the steps, out of the house, towards the sea, and as I rolled I touched my arms and legs and felt a thin layer of fur.

———————

The kitchen carpet was the worst place to find yourself in our house – *on* the kitchen carpet that is, *on top of*, or *close to*, or *anywhere near* – because the kitchen carpet was always filthy, caked in dirt. Disgusting, my brother said, and he meant like the house Mr and Mrs Twit live in where they throw all their cold and congealed spaghetti. Like the bottom of a sewer, like the place where rats get stuck, like the place where all the bits of food and hair and unwanted vegetables and cold bits of greasy potato and scraggy bits of toenails and skin *festered*, said my brother, who was copying Mum, because 'festered' wasn't his word.

Festered! Festered! Festered! Jane Eyre festered on the floor of the Red Room. Jane Eyre festered all alone. *To fester*: to *feel the opposite* of going to a festival or fête, or a birthday party; quite *the opposite* of a sunny day on the green in the summer with Aunt Jayne and her billowing skirts and strong calves; very much *the opposite* of a lovely day outside on the beach with an ice-cream cone at the end of it.

To fester is to stay indoors all day with no possibility of a walk. To fester is to peer through the downstairs front-room window and wonder why no one ever came up the steps. To fester is to retreat inside dark spaces, the cellar, the bathroom, my mum's bedroom, the downstairs kitchen.

To fester is to feel shame, and I did. I felt ashamed of my house, I felt ashamed of us and of what we were hiding: the damp and the fury and the filth; the dirty past; Poor Sue, her body tumbling down the stairs, behind the locked door; the door at the top of the stairs; the white door that closed us off, the door that sealed us off.

And seals, Mum says, are hard to break. You need brute force, a strong wrist. You need to break through the trapped air, the vacuum, that space where no one goes. In order to break the seal you have to first swallow hard and make your best fist.

That's why leaving anywhere you've been all your life is so hard, breaking open the seal. I don't know how to describe it, but it's like getting rid of a big lump that has been stuck in your throat for years, that apple, Adam's apple, the apple that got stuck in his throat right at the beginning, when everything went wrong, when Eve heeded the Serpent's wicked words and went behind Adam's back like a sneaky little devil without even washing her hands first, said John Reed to Jane Eyre as he slapped her. Leaving is like that: it's getting a big slap on your face and a hard knock on your head. It's John Reed knocking Jane Eyre sideways and pushing her onto the floor, then snatching her book from her hands, her book of birds,

Bewick's Book of Birds, *you beast, you rotten beast, you filthy rotten beast, give it back, give it back now! Send her away, Mama! Send her away! Lock her up, Mama! Lock her up! She's filth. Pure filth.*

When I found myself on the kitchen carpet I knew it was the end: the end of everything. I had broken through the white door and fallen down the stairs. At the bottom of the stairs my aunt was waiting to cover my body with a white sheet. Sometime after nightfall she would bury me at the bottom of the garden along with all the other lost souls.

And I knew the moment my aunt got down on her knees and put her hands together that it was over, because she'd begun to pray, and her praying was dark and dreadful. The sounds were hard and sharp and stuck in her throat. She was cawing. 'Cri-Cri-Cri-Cri.' Cri-de-ker, kri-de-ker, kri-de-ker. My aunt was turning into a bird, a crow, a big black crow with a shiny head and a sharp beak and a neck that swivelled towards me and she opened her beak and cawed, sharp words, stuck words, words stuck in her throat, bits of apple covered in skin, my skin. My aunt was ripping at my skin with her sharp beak and all the time she was cawing sharp sounds, like knives. She was peeling her apple, she was taking the apple out from her throat where it was stuck and she was pushing it down my throat: her words, her sounds, her sharp knife, her arrows of God.

———

Five o' clock had hardly struck on the morning of the 19th of January when Bessie brought a candle into my closet and found me already up and nearly dressed ... I was to leave Gateshead that day by a coach which passed the lodge gates at six a.m.

(*Jane Eyre*)

A few days later an ambulance came and took me away. Two men picked me up and carried me off as though I weighed nothing at all. They laid me on a white stretcher as if I was one of the birds Washington (my cat) had caught in his mouth and mauled at. They were nice men. They spoke to me as though everything was normal, this carrying out of bodies, dead or alive, for a nice trip to the seaside.

But I knew I was being carried away to Coventry in an ambulance. I lay back and listened.

'Lie back now, dear, and feel the sun on your face. This one's nice and comfy, not too bumpy. Good suspension. Not like the other one. It rattled the bones something awful.'

'What sort of place is this, then, Jim? Ever heard of it?'

'No idea, mate. Never heard of it. A kids' home, I think. You know, for if they're in a spot of trouble.'

'What do they do with them there, then?'

'No idea, mate. No idea. Poor little buggers.'

'She came to me from the orphanage,' Miss Marple tells Inspector Neele. 'Gladys Martin came to me from St Faith's. She was a poor little thing. Easily led. Gladys was so easily taken in. She had no family you see, Inspector, and a girl with no living relations is a poor thing indeed. It makes you very vulnerable. Gladys was desperate for someone to tell her what to do. She was always hiding things, things about her past, things she felt ashamed of … her best friend Sue was like that, Sue Blunt. Sue was another poor thing. Completely taken in by religion.'

Miss Marple suddenly stopped for a moment and looked out the window at the grey sky. The birds were gathering in clumps on the trees. She turned back to the inspector, who was drumming his fingers on the desk and looking rather puzzled. The name Sue Blunt, he thought, rang faint bells. But the old lady hadn't finished.

'Religion can cover a lot of holes, Inspector. It promises a lot of things. New life, a whole new life, and if your life here on earth isn't up to much, well, for a girl like Sue Blunt, that can be very alluring.'

30

COLWOOD

The night passed rapidly. I was too tired even to dream;
I only awoke once to hear the wind rave in furious gusts,
and the rain fall in torrents … when I again unclosed my
eyes, a loud bell was ringing; the girls were up and
dressing; day had not yet begun to dawn, and a
rushlight or two burned in the room. I too rose reluctantly;
it was bitter cold, and I dressed as well as I could for
shivering.

(*Jane Eyre*)

By the time I got to Colwood I knew that feeling is what
makes you ill, too much feeling. Feeling is what made Mum
lie in bed all day; feeling is what made my aunt scream and
shout; feeling is what made Jane Eyre run away from
Thornfield on her wedding night; feeling is what kept Mr
Rochester with his head in his hands locked up in the library
with no fire lit.

Feeling is what led me to Colwood. I didn't stay at Colwood
for as long as Jane stays at Lowood School (half her young life

at least), but it was months, and in the end, years. After a while I lost count. In between there were other places, other homes that weren't homes, other Thornfields and Gateshead Halls with granite outlooks and gloomy clouds; places in which there was never a possibility of taking a walk that day or any other. But I don't like to think about it too much, because none of those places was suitable for a girl like Jane Eyre.

Colwood was a place of lost days, days that existed only inside doctors' notes. And those sorts of notes never read well. How could they? Outside of books, nothing much happens. Most of life is boring, which is why you have to make some of it up.

When I think of Colwood I remember nothing except the ringing of the bell and the early-morning feel of cold linoleum on my feet. And then I see the black bars at the window. It's hard to describe how it feels to live behind closed windows, with barely a hint of wind or air, with nothing fresh hitting your cheek. No sharp sting. Nothing real or alive or racing. Life without a heartbeat.

———————

Every morning at 7.30 a bell rang to wake us up. Soon after, someone began yelling. That was the nurse, the nurse who wore squeaky shoes and always said the same thing over and over again: 'Wakey, wakey, rise and shine, into the shower, quick, hop, you morning beauties, breakfast at eight, you know the routine.'

Nurses like to keep routines. They like to keep notes; and keeping notes, I realised, is quite dull, unless you notice very particular things and then use precisely the right words.

The nurse: who sometimes was a man with thinning hair and sometimes a woman with blonde hair and a ponytail, and sometimes black and called Janet. I gave them all words, these nurses who weren't nurses (because nurses always wear uniform). *The nurse with thinning hair*, the man that is, I would say that he was *disconsolate* (he could not be consoled or comforted; he didn't like life or living). He was like Mr Rochester after Jane leaves him, all stooped over and without his hat on. Jane Eyre is never disconsolate, except perhaps when she is wandering over the heath looking for some shelter. Miss Marple isn't disconsolate. She's lived too long for that.

The nurse with the blonde ponytail was *cheerful*, and *cheerful people* always make you feel better. She was cheerful even inside Colwood because she liked children and teenagers and because, I think, she had just *decided to be that way. Cheerful people have decided that being cheerful is a good way to be.* She walked down the dark corridor at 7.30 a.m. and her ponytail swung and her hips moved slightly left to right, and I thought she looked like a *cheerful pony* trotting around her pen. Our pen.

The black nurse was *difficult*. It's hard to give her only one word. She needed more. She was bitter on the outside like a sharp fruit – a tangy orange – which she peeled every morning at breakfast. Then she was slow and serene. *Deliberate*. That is a good word for Janet. She was *slow and deliberate*, like Janet from my first reading book, but not Janet, the girl with blonde hair I never really liked, but the words on the page *about* Janet. Those words were slow and deliberate because they were meant to help us read, but I found them boring because they were always the same words. Because Janet inside the book was always predictable.

Janet in real life wasn't boring, she was *interesting, intriguing*, and sometimes *she was frightening*. It was the way she said things and then did them, with *no hesitation*. When I wanted to eat an apple instead of a banana she told me that I had no choice except the banana. She said it just like that. 'There is no choice.' I couldn't tell her that I wanted to eat an apple because they are crisp and refreshing, like drinking sweet water, and that apples also clean your teeth. I also didn't want to eat a banana just then because they made me miss James and the Bahamas, but above all because my aunt had made me eat a banana one morning by force.

———————

I feared nothing but interruption, and that came too soon. The breakfast-room door opened. 'Boh! Madam Mope!' cried the voice of John Reed.

(*Jane Eyre*)

That morning had been dark with storm clouds, and when I looked out the window I knew there was no possibility of taking a walk that day. I had been grounded and spent the morning in my room. That morning I feared nothing but interruption, which soon and inexorably came. After an hour or so, after the house had become still and quiet, after the school bell had rung, I heard the door open and someone push past the sticky door handle. I saw a shadow fall across the net curtains.

My aunt was in the room. I hid beneath my covers with a book over my head hoping that the pages would turn into wings.

'If you don't sit still, you must be tied down,' said Bessie. 'Miss Abbot, lend me your garters. She will break mine directly.' My aunt didn't tie me down, but after a while, after some polite speaking and cajoling, after the slow run-up, the careful unpeeling, the slow and deliberate movement of hands, my aunt put her hands on my mouth and forced it open. She stuffed the banana in, and when I felt its sweet soggy wet taste against my teeth, the teeth I pulled down like bars, I spat it out and it fell to the ground and I looked down at it lying on the carpet, as though it were my worst enemy, because it came from my aunt, and for no other reason.

I was conscious that a moment's mutiny had already rendered me liable to strange penalties, and I resisted all the way. And as I resisted, I thought of James and his dad and the bananas they shipped over from the Bahamas falling to the bottom of the sea, because sometimes bananas sink, especially if there is a storm over the Caribbean and the sailors are all sick. Then, inexorably, without any doubt at all, the bananas and the sailors and the entire ship are drowned by the dark-eyed waves.

> My heart beat thick, my head grew hot; a sound filled my ears, which I deemed the rushing of wings: someone near me; I was oppressed, suffocated: endurance broke down – I uttered a wild, involuntary cry.
>
> (*Jane Eyre*)

———————

As a general rule, I don't think you should do anything by force. If you do, it is bound to breed resentment or hate or illness; you are sure to cause a scene, produce a wild, involuntary cry. But none of this bothered Janet, the black nurse, whose family once came from Jamaica. I first met Janet the day she came into my dormitory and put her cold clammy hands on me and asked me to strip so she could insert something into me from behind. I first met Janet the day she asked me to lie down on the bed inside my dormitory, the room I slept in with three walls, not four, so you couldn't really call it a room – perhaps *a space*. A room is closed off and private; there are no prying eyes; there is a door. Our dormitories were made only for prying and peeking and listening in because we were observed from dawn to midnight, from midnight to dawn. In our dormitories, we were strange wild seafowl from solitary promontories whose habits had to be noted down and known. So there were bars on the window to keep us from flying off. Bars locked us in night and day, day and night. I never once saw the moon from my dormitory window, nor the sun. The God of Wind and Rain, the Sun and the Stars, was nowhere to be seen. '*Jane, I don't like cavillers or questioners; besides, there is something truly forbidding in a child taking up her elders in that manner. Be seated somewhere; and until you can speak pleasantly, remain silent.*'

I first met Janet the day she walked into my dormitory and told me things about my body, private things, things that should never be said out loud. She said them with such calm conviction that there was no questioning her. Janet *didn't like cavillers or questioners*, and so there was no possibility of further enquiry. I simply consented. I consented against my will because with Janet there was never any shouting and there was never any choice. Janet was the calm after the storm, but with Janet you never even saw the storm. By the time Janet arrived the storm had been and gone. All that remained were a few spare facts, the facts of life, the physical facts, because *Janet only ever spoke about physical things*. She never discussed psychology much. Psychology was like a storm; it soon passes over. But when Janet spoke about bodies, well, these were just basic facts – like the fact that you can't buy strawberries in winter and that celery can be eaten both cooked and raw. If you do eat it raw, it is better with salt, but too much salt will ruin it.

Janet was someone to be afraid of because she never gave much away. People like that are always frightening, you might say *troubling* or *disconcerting*. You can't get in. The latch is always down. Janet didn't let you ask questions, and for someone like me that was a very hard thing. Janet refused questions. All she would talk about was food, what food was good for you and what wasn't, while she slowly peeled her orange in front of you and expected you to wait for her. There was no getting around Janet. She had seen it all before, the cavillers and questioners, the Caribbean storms, the shipwrecks.

Janet was no Bertha Mason, though they came from the same place. With Janet, there was a lot of history, but I was never allowed to know it. Her history was shut away as tightly as the air inside Colwood. Janet was an air-sealed casket. She had been shipped overseas years ago and she was never coming back.

But deep down I knew that Janet was also just tired. She was *desultory*, that was another word for her: *fatigued*, worn out, spent, indifferent, too calm for words. *Because Janet had given up on most words.* She hated explanations. Those weren't needed. Not now. It was too late. Better to say as little as possible. Just state the facts, calmly and slowly, and the world will keep turning with you.

And the facts were these: that Janet had other children to care for, not us. We were not her *main concern*, not now, not ever. Janet had other burdens to bear, which is why she was so deliberate about everything she did. Her heart and mind were elsewhere, back in Jamaica with her family, singing to the low moon. In Jamaica, Janet had an ageing mother slowly climbing the walls, or a lover dying in a high room.

31

AN ANGRY GOBLIN'S CELL

One night I had been awakened by her yells – (since the
medical profession had pronounced her mad, she had of
course been shut up) – it was a fiery West-Indian night;
one of the description that frequently precede the
hurricanes of those climates: being unable to sleep in bed, I
got up and opened the window.

(Jane Eyre)

One night in Colwood I had a dream. It's a dream I had had
before and have had several times since. In my dream, I see
Poor Sue clinging like a lizard to a windowpane. The window
is hot and sweaty and the glass is dark. Pressed to the pane I
see a pair of beady eyes and a squashed nose. She has no hair.
Her fur is gone and her eyes are bulging, so full of blood they
are about to burst.

Behind her sits a woman in a white veil. The veil covers the
woman's mouth, but her mouth is moving. The veil is going
inside her mouth and the woman is chewing the veil. Her
teeth are cutting through the white linen. Her tongue is

— 224 —

moving as fast as a serpent's tongue and the tongue is getting longer and longer and licking up the air.

And on the air are black flies, hundreds and hundreds of flies, and the flies are dying. They are dying on top of the serpent's tongue, black flies rolling over on their wings and crushing themselves to death. And there is the smell of something bad, the stench of a corpse, and the corpse is rotting. The corpse is rotting beneath the window, at the bottom of the garden, where Verity lay. And in my dream, I watch the lizard and it crawls out of the window and along the garden path, across the sun-parched grass on the lawn, towards the dark soil around the rubbish bins that hasn't seen water since that hot summer, long ago, when they say old people fell fainting from windows with the heat.

In Jamaica, at least, Mr Rochester could open the window to clear out the smell and release the heat. But in Colwood you could not. In Jamaica you opened windows to let in the storm. Opening windows relieves tension: atmosphere, scudding clouds, whipping rain, bad dreams. But open windows were forbidden at Colwood; so the only way to relieve tension was to shout and scream, and my dream at least made me scream.

To England, then, I conveyed her: a fearful voyage I had with such a monster in the vessel. Glad was I when I at last got her to Thornfield, and saw her safely lodged in that third story room, of whose secret inner cabinet she has now for ten years made a wild beast's den – a goblin's cell.

(*Jane Eyre*)

I am starting to sound like an adult. This is what happens when you have adults watching over you all day and all night, adults looking down on you, even in your sleep. At Colwood, Mr Murdstone was constantly peering at me from the corner of the room as I went about my business; Mr Brocklehurst was staring at me from the front of the schoolroom with his tall purple hat, Mr Brocklehurst *wrapped in a cloud of silvery plumage*; Mr Murdstone with his furious visage glaring at me from across the room. *I could have done very well without the Murdstones*, says David Copperfield, *but the influence of the Murdstones upon me was like the fascination of two snakes on a wretched young bird.*

And whatever Bertha Mason must have felt under the calm, cool gaze of Grace Poole, I felt too. Because at Colwood we were all beasts of one kind or another: goblins and fairy folk, witches and elves. But I'm only going to tell you about one of these strange things, because Tracy White, or Trace as we called her, was one of the strangest of all.

Trace was usually seen with socks around her ankles. No one had ever told her about nylons. When I met her, I knew that Trace was one of Miss Marple's poor things. She was the adenoidal type – Gladys Martin speaking through her nose – and I felt sorry for her. Mum says you shouldn't feel sorry for people. Well, I didn't *only* feel sorry for Trace. I liked her too, because she was funny and plain-spoken. She knew what she liked; she knew what she loved. And isn't that the main thing?

———

When Inspector Neele goes to inspect Gladys Martin's room at Yewtree Lodge he finds an untidy and slovenly space. 'Slovenly' is his word for it. Gladys Martin, he decides, may have been trained well as a maid, but in her personal life her habits were chaotic and slovenly.

'Slovenly' is a cruel word to use for Gladys. Slovenly suggests 'sluttish'. Gladys, the inspector suggests, might be found with her nylons down. When he goes through her things he finds cheap knick-knacks: a small collection of shells bound inside a soiled handkerchief and a Polaroid shot of Gladys beaming with two other girls dressed in waitresses' uniforms behind a countertop. Girls like Tracy White.

Trace was fifteen or sixteen, and the first thing you noticed about her was that she had large breasts. You noticed partly because she was short, but also because she wore tight white T-shirts. On her bottom half she wore flared skirts, the sort of skirts I wore to school, skirts that puffed up behind like a balloon.

No one knew why Trace was at Colwood. Perhaps she had refused to go to school; she did tell me once that she had been told she had to wash more and that people had complained about her clothes. But Trace wasn't one of the self-harming girls. No, Trace was always cheerful. Trace wanted to be a pop star. She was practising for *Top of the Pops*.

'There's a bit in me head,' she said to me one morning. 'There's a bit stuck in me head. Sal, I can't get it out. It's crawlin' round me head. Madonna. It's all 'er fault. I can't get her outta me head.'

'Who, Tracy? Who's stuck in your head?'

'Bleedin' Madonna.'

And suddenly Trace began whirling round and round on the shiny floor with her arms wide open like a little girl twirling a hula hoop on the beach, a little girl catching at her ball, a little girl who had never been to school and couldn't read, a little girl who knew only some of the words to pop songs.

Spinning round and round,
She's in trouble …
You'd better say a prayer
For the girl in trouble,
The girl in lots of trouble.

Years later, I found Trace inside another book, a book by a man called John Fowles. One of the characters in that book is the spit of Trace, so close in fact that when I read it after all those years I couldn't stop crying. I shook and shook because I knew I'd found her, Trace that is, and this is her story.

A man finds a young girl in a cinema and takes her back to his flat. She is dressed in an old man's duffle coat, a dirty grey sweater and some baggy jeans. The girl snuffles all the time and she has dirty fingernails. The girl, whose name is something like Janey or Janine, but let's call her Sue, pretends to be twenty-four, but really she's seventeen, and she's never slept with a man before. But she'd like to.

But the man, let's call him David, or Dave, doesn't want to sleep with her, so they agree to be friends. They muddle along for a while, some nights sharing the same bed. Dave is slightly annoyed at Sue's snuffling about and her filthy fingernails and her running off to attend strange meetings about the Holy Spirit. But he feels something for her nonetheless. It's hard not to feel something for Poor Sue.

Then one day Dave finds his bed empty. Sue has gone. He looks all over London for her but he can't find her in any of her usual haunts: the Red Cross charity shop near Marylebone, the café where they sell chips for 20p, the church hall where she goes on Saturday mornings early to get all the bargains, the Save the Children shop off Notting Hill High Street. No matter where he looks he can't find the girl who slurps her tea and squeezes chips with her filthy fingernails, the girl whose hair is always in her face and whose duffle coat carries bits of mud and leaves around the hem (she sometimes sleeps in Kensington Gardens). That girl, Sue, who has a thick Glaswegian accent and chipmunk cheeks, David tells the police, goes missing one day from his bed. He knows she's been there because he can smell the damp outside on his sheets. He can see the shape of her furry hood. That girl, who he never sees again.

The girl I knew, the girl called Trace, was spotty and dumpy round the middle. She was short and untidy. That's what I'd tell the police anyway, because to say anything else wouldn't be truthful. Her clothes never fitted or matched, so things were always spilling out: bits of blouse, bits of belly, bits of saggy underwear. And because Trace wore charity-shop clothes, clothes she never washed, she always smelled bad.

'Urgh, Trace, you fucking stinking old woman ... gross ... get away. You smell like a pig, you fat stinking pig. Go and have a bath!'

Poor Trace. All she ever wanted was for the boys to notice her, so whenever she could get out of Colwood she went to the charity shops to find more clothes to make herself look nice.

Trace loved charity shops. They were her passion. She went to charity shops with plastic bags stuffed inside her dress. But she could only afford the things she found on the sale rail. The sale rail was her favourite thing. She dreamed of that rail. She dreamed of it day and night.

'Sal, I found a *gorgeous* blouse for 50p, nipped in round the breasts. Look, it holds me in nice and tight ... shows off my best part ... Look, Sal, look!'

Trace was always making me look. I had to look and look and then make nice comments about her breasts and bum. Nothing else. Always her breasts and bum.

'Do you think this blouse goes with my jeans? I'm not very good in jeans. I need to be nice and thin like you ... Mind you, you're too thin. You don't have any boobs. At least I've got those. You need to get a pair, you know. It's what boys like. Then, when you get them, when you get a bit of weight on yer – you do need a bit of weight on yer, you know – yer need to show them off as much as possible. I can get yer something if you like, from the sale rail.

Yer need to think about what will make you look nice and sexy, Sal, because boys like yer to look sexy … But you've got to grow a pair first. You can't go out looking like that!'

Trace was always talking about going out *looking like that*. She spent most of her time thinking about this. Going out looking like something was the most important thing to her, and whenever she could she practised her Madonna routines in her dorm, because she believed Madonna was the sexiest woman in the world and if she could only twist and turn and writhe like Madonna then the boys would come running. So she sang Madonna songs at the top of her lungs and drove all of us crazy.

'Bloody hell, shut up won't you, Trace? Stop that fucking racket! What the fuck is wrong with you? You're not bloody Madonna, all right? You're not even close. *Not even close*, Trace. Quit that fucking racket and wake up!' Sharon Pointer. It was always Sharon Pointer.

But through the walls Trace was twisting and turning; she was saying her pop prayers.

In your prayers, I will take you there, say your prayers, and I will take you there …

'In your dreams, Trace, in your dreams. Now shut the fuck up!'

———

The truth is, no one wanted Trace. They'd want her even less if they knew a thing or two. For one thing, her mother lay in a creaky bed in a bedsit in Hastings on Sea and pointed at whatever she wanted, because her mother couldn't speak. She could only point with her fat greasy fingers, fingers she filled with greasy chips, chips she sucked on like sweets, Trace told me. And when you have a mother like that, a mother who doesn't notice you, a mother who can't notice you, and a father who was never known, a father who might as well have been a piece of square yellow Lego for all Trace cared, a Lego man with no clothes, a Lego man she couldn't bleedin' find in the heap of sticky plastic cubes she sifted through at the back of the charity shop.

Trace was always looking for men. 'He's *gorgeous*,' she said every morning before breakfast about the man in uniform serving up cold baked beans in metal trays, the man who didn't once look back at her, the man who never once smiled. 'He's bleedin' gorgeous!'

Trace was the first girl I knew to use that word about a man. *Gorgeous*, I mean. I don't know where she got it from, that word for men.

How were men *gorgeous*, exactly? *Gorgeous* was for lovely sea views, for scones and cream, for Victoria sponge cake, for Mum's favourite lacy white dress, maybe for Princess Di. *Gorgeous* was for my mother before she had had children. *Gorgeous* was for the floral fabric she'd spied in Bentalls department store in Worthing, the rose-covered fabric she was hoping would come on sale soon, the fabric she took a sample of and kept in her bedroom drawer. *Gorgeous* was never for men.

Of course I knew Trace was looking for a life with something gorgeous in it, because so far she hadn't got much to go on.

'Mum stays in bed all day,' she told me one morning at breakfast. 'She can't get up. Her ankles are too fat. I have to make the beans all the time.'

'Make the beans?'

'Baked beans. Bleedin' baked beans. What do you fink?'

Trace would only eat baked beans on toast or toast and nothing else. On the days when beans weren't served she threw a fit.

'Beans, mate! Where are the bloody beans?' she yelled to the canteen staff.

'None today, Trace. We'll bring them up tomorrow.'

'I'm not eating peas. It looks like sick. You've puked all over 'em. I'm not touchin' em. I'm not! I'm not! I'm not eating disgusting puke!'

Trace turned her small, shaking body towards the plastic swing doors of the dining hall and banged right through them. 'Bloody owwww. Bloody hell. Owwww! Owwww!'

The next day she was locked in a side room and I didn't see her for days. Maybe weeks.

32

THE STORY OF SUE

(ANOTHER SHORT CHAPTER)

Only time will heal, people say. Only time will heal the bad things, bring the ivy back over the wall. Because ivy provides good cover, for garden blemishes and broken bricks, for holes in the wall. *Ivy can cover a multitude of sins*, says Mum, *but you need to keep an eye on it, it'll soon take over. Ivy is strong as an ox at the roots … it needs a good strong wall.*

I've spent several years inside walls – two years inside Colwood and more elsewhere – so I've thought a lot about walls and what they do to people, and what people do with walls.

> The garden was a wide inclosure, surrounded with walls so
> high as to exclude every glimpse of prospect.

> *(Jane Eyre)*

Mum loved the old brick wall that ran along the edge of our garden, between the Greens' house on one side and the Sturgesses' on the other. For years she ran her roses along that crumbling red brick: Clementine and Josephine, Dorothy and Matilda, Valerie and Natalie. Year in and year out her beloved girls came back to report on the weather, the conditions of the soil, the difficulty of that hot summer. Much later, when she had to leave her beloved garden behind, those girls caused her a great deal of trouble.

Quite an operation, she told Maze. *The roots are so deep, so stubborn, I had to draw them out with pliers and wire. In the end I had to borrow a drill from the council.*

When I heard Mum speak of her stubborn girls I thought of Betsey Trotwood and her beloved piece of turf. Betsey would never ever budge; she would always be on the edge of that chalky cliff, peering out of the window at her precious bit of green; because people go mad for their little bit of turf. The thought of losing it nearly sends them over the edge; because inside that small patch of grass are stored all the hopes and dreams of the never-forgotten past and the forever-hoped-for future. *Janet, Donkeys! Janet! Donkeys!* Always and forever!

———————

Old stories are stubborn. You can nip and prune and cut back a bit, but you can't easily shift their roots. The story of Sue is very stubborn. It runs deep.

But sometimes, if you're listening for it, unexpected infor-mation comes your way. Quite out of the blue, someone will tell you something you didn't know, and suddenly it dawns on you that the noises in the attic come from a living person, not a ghost.

Once upon a time and quite out of the blue I learned that Sue was a real person too. Years later, quite unexpectedly, I was reminded of this by Someone's Mother. Such things usually come from aunts or mothers, new information that is, a quick reversal in fortune.

Look at Aunt Reed. Just before she dies she summons Jane Eyre to her. It turns out that Mrs Reed of Gateshead House, Jane's aunt, has been concealing a very important fact:

'Go to my dressing-case, open it, and take out a letter you will see there.'

I obeyed her directions. 'Read the letter,' she said.

It was short and thus conceived: –

'Madam, – will you have the goodness to send me the address of my niece, Jane Eyre, and tell me how she is? It is my intention to write shortly and desire her to come to Madeira. Providence has blessed my endeavours to secure a competency; and as I am unmarried and childless, I wish to adopt her during my life, and bequeath her at my death whatever I may have to leave. – I am, Madam, &c.'.,

(JOHN EYRE, Madeira)

What this means is that Jane Eyre is no longer an orphan; she will no longer be kept below stairs. Instead, she will wear satin dresses and put ribbons in her hair. Some mornings she will lie late in bed and look out at the sun. She will dangle her toes over the edge of the bed and smile.

———————

Sue was an orphan too. Someone's Mother told me this. They'd been friends at school. When they were young women, they trained together to be midwives. Sometime in the 1960s, in Angmering on Sea, Sue was pulling babies from bellies with Someone's Mother. But then Someone's Mother went off to marry and Sue was left behind pulling babies and praying to God in a dingy front room in Sussex. That's when Sue met the woman in the white veil and the black rocks began flying.

There are still gaps in the story, several missing bricks, but I do know that Sue was taken away. She was kept in an attic room; she was locked in a side room, all white and covered in sheets. And that's when Sue began screaming, yelling like a banshee. Soon after, the black rocks began to fly.

33

CROSSING THE MEADOW

When Jane returns to Thornfield Hall she finds a blackened ruin. It is a winter's evening and the clouds are drawing in. The weathermen speak of gales. There is frost on the church porch.

'My first view of it shall be in front,' Jane says to herself as she crosses the fields and meadows, as she passes through the woods, as she spies the village church, as she sees the dark hulk of Thornfield Hall looming in the distance. 'It looks best from the front, its bold battlements strike the eye … I shall be filled with wonder.'

But what comes is not wonder, only black shadows and ruin. The battlements have crumbled. Crows are building their nests among the grey stone. Jane looks up, and instead of tall towers and proud crests, sees only fallen men. Thornfield is burned to the ground.

Jane's first life is over. This is the beginning of her second. She sits down on the mossy ground and looks around. In the cold morning air she takes a deep breath and turns back towards the black battlements.

Starting a second life is hard. Fairy godmothers can be a big help, but at some point you have to face facts, the long gap between leaving and returning. Nothing will ever be the same again.

But then, one day, you find yourself walking through an English village, the village you once called home, when something quite familiar meets your eye. It is the lineaments of a face, the character of a landscape you once knew, and you know you are near your bourne.

Once more on the road to Thornfield … I felt like the messenger-pigeon flying home … Yes, I knew the character of this landscape: I was sure we were near my bourne.

You may go away, but where you were born, or where you were borne from, remains the same. When Jane returns to Thornfield she finds Mrs Fairfax, the housekeeper, still there, Mrs Fairfax as sturdy as the gatepost she climbs over.

'I suppose you are a stranger in these parts, or you would have heard what happened last autumn, – Thornfield Hall is quite a ruin: it was burnt down just about harvest-time. A dreadful calamity!'

Jane listens, and her body shivers with fear. Old Jane is dead; a new Jane must begin. As she crosses the long stretch of meadow that surrounds her first home, her mind strays towards the image that has haunted her all these years.

Every place you've lived in has something you carry with you. For me, that's the painting in the dining hall at Colwood above the tables where we ate. It is a picture of a child holding a white dove. The child is clinging to the dove; he is squeezing the dove tight, because the child is frightened. He has wandered from his cot, out into the meadow. The morning grass is wet and sodden. It is summer and the earth is warm; there are buttercups and daisies on the ground. But the child can hear his mother's voice; she is telling the story of the fairies, the fairies that live forever. The child hears the story and longs to fly as they do, so he carries on, across the meadow.

A strong wind begins to blow and the corners of her white blanket lift. The child looks up and sees the dove. The dove will show him how to fly! The dove will take him to the fairies! So the child with the white blanket runs across the meadow and the clouds puff and blow, puff and blow, and the child lifts up his arms and sails into the sky.

———————

Of all the records we played as children, my favourite was the story by a man called Prokofiev of *Peter and the Wolf*. I loved the sound of Peter running out into the meadow, Peter soaring high on the strings, Peter carefree and running through his grandfather's gate out into the wide, green world.

Shh! It's about to start. Lie still, won't you? said my brother. *The man is about to begin!*

Early one morning Peter goes out into the big green meadow. He meets a little bird in the tree. Before long the bird becomes his friend; the bird, she says, will teach him how to fly.

'What kind of a bird are you if you can't fly?' the little bird says. Soon after, a duck comes along, and the duck asks the little bird, 'What kind of bird are you if you can't swim?'

The music grows louder, and the duck starts to waggle about. He doesn't notice the clever cat creeping through the grass on her velvet paws. But Peter sees her coming, and he shouts 'Out! Out! Out cat! Out!'

'Out! Out! Out!' My brother jumped up and screamed. 'Out cat, out! Out! Out! The wolf is coming, the wolf is coming, the wolf is coming! You stupid cat, you stupid cat! The wolf is coming! Can't you see? Run away, run away, run away!'

'Not yet!' The grandfather has to come out first, and he will shut the gate so the wolf can't get in. 'Shut the door, Peter, shut the door. Shhh! She'll hear … Shhh!'

'It's a dangerous place. If a wolf were to come out of the forest, then what would you do?'

'Peter! Sit down and be quiet. She'll come downstairs if you carry on like that.'

Peter paid no attention to his grandfather's words, because boys like him are not afraid of wolves.

But grandfather took Peter by the hand, locked the gate, and led him home.

'Just in the nick of time,' Mum said as she passed by the door. 'Now close the door. You'll wake Di.'

The horns blared. I looked up towards the ceiling; the chandelier was shaking ever so slightly.

'Shh! She's awake,' I said. 'Shhh!'

The wolf is coming and the duck is running away. But the duck can't run fast enough because she's fat and the wolf has fast, greedy eyes and his eyes are tearing towards the fluffy white duck. Now the wolf is slinking along the ground, but the duck doesn't see the wolf coming, because she is waddling about and arguing with the bird.

'Shh! Peter! Shh! Shhh!'

The horns are getting louder and louder. They are so loud I can hear them inside my ear. Blah! Blah! Blah! Blah! Blast! Blast! Blast! Blast and balderdash! Shut up, you awful little swines! Shut up! For God's sake, shut up! Some of us are trying to sleep! Switch that racket off! For Pete's sake switch it off!

But Peter wasn't afraid. Boys like him are not afraid of wolves. He went back into his grandfather's house and found a piece of rope and went back out into the meadow. He climbed the tallest tree he could find and wrapped the rope around his wrist and then his middle until he had made a long lasso. Peter picked up his lasso and put it over his shoulders; he inched closer along the branch.

Then suddenly a sound started up behind him. *Tweet, tweet, tweet, tweet!* It was the voice of the little bird. Silly little bird, thought Peter. She'll get herself killed. Shh! Shh!

But the bird was cleverer than the wolf, and stayed up high in the tree among the branches. And when Peter saw that the little bird was safe, he lowered his lasso close to the ground and dangled it behind the tree. And when the greedy wolf came close to the tree Peter said to the little bird, *'Tweet, tweet, little bird, tweet, tweet, tweet,'* and the little bird tweeted with all her heart. Then just as the wolf caught sight of him, Peter pulled hard on the lasso.

Tweet tweet said the little bird, Tweet tweet tweet.

———————

One summer when we were hot and bothered and bored my brothers and I invented a game. We called it 'Tweet tweet'. The rule was that you had to pass from one room to another without ever putting a foot on the ground. 'Even a toe counts,' said my brothers, 'even your little toe touching the ground!'

So we climbed across the kitchen table and jumped towards the sink and climbed out through the window on all fours. Then we edged our way along the drainpipe, clinging with bare toes, to the bathroom at the back of the house. When I caught my cotton petticoat on the window ledge, and the force of it dragged me to the floor, my brothers yelled, 'The big bad wolf has got you … You're out! You're out! The big bad wolf has got his teeth out! You're out! You're out!' And I sat on the floor and went *Tweet, tweet tweet, tweet tweet tweet* but my brothers said it was too late for that. Wolves don't wait for little birds. If a little bird falls from the tree they gobble it up.

———————

Sometime in the winter of 1986 I fell from my tree. But in truth, I made myself fall. I did it sitting on a hospital bed with a clipboard in my hand and a woman sitting next to me on a plastic chair. The woman handed me the clipboard with a form attached to it and explained that if I did this, if I signed the form, then I would never have to go home again. I would have to go somewhere, but she wasn't quite sure where yet. I could stay in Colwood for a few more months, but I couldn't stay here forever. I was going to have to go into care.

'Going into Care,' explained the woman on the plastic chair, meant that Social Services were now in charge of me. They had to find me somewhere to live. They'd tried a few homes, but everything was full. I'd have to be patient.

'Turn the page over,' said the lady. On the other side of the form there was a name and a signature: Angela Christine Bayley. Date of Birth: 18 December 1947. I peered at the date, and for the first time I realised how old my mother was. I was fourteen. My mother was nearly forty. She was nearly three times my age. My mother didn't look young or old, I thought, only pale.

I looked down and I could see her pale face floating through the form. Then I saw her mouth; it was moving.

'Up, up and away, in my beautiful balloon.'

Mum sang that song on Sundays while she was doing her hair.

'Nancy's best song. Not a patch on her dad, but not a bad effort. Middle of the road, sweet voice. The Americans like it.'

My mother's mouth was moving through the long, wide vowels. She liked vowels. Vowels should linger and stay, she said. Vowels were to be savoured. 'Open your mouth and speak properly. Pronounce your vowels, for goodness' sake!'

My mother's mouth is moving slowly around her coffee cup. She is sipping her coffee slowly and gently. Now my mother's mouth is open; it is as wide as the brim of her cup. 'Sa-lly-Sa-man-tha-M-ary-Bay-ley … If Margaret Thatcher can learn to speak properly, so can we.'

'Have you read it properly, Sally?' asked the lady on the plastic chair. I jumped. 'Your mother has consented. She's signed the form.'

My hands trembled. 'It doesn't say anything about a home. Where will I live?'

'We don't know yet. We'll need to find somewhere. It may take a few weeks. I'm trying to find somewhere suitable. It may not be *perfectly* suitable to begin with … or purr-fect-ly beautiful.'

'Suitable,' said Mrs Rutherford. '"Sue" as in "zoo", but with an "s". "Sue-ta-ble". *Sue-ta-ble* is one of those words you need to make the most of. There will be many occasions when you will think something is not quite sue-tar-bull. *Not quite the thing … no thank you, I'd rather not.*'

'I'd rather not go anywhere that wasn't suitable. I'd rather stay here. I've got used to it.'

'You can't stay here. We need to find something longer-term.'

'How long? How long are you sending me away for? The last time I was sent away they told me it would be a little holiday. It turned out to be a year and three months, nearly four … which wasn't very suitable.'

'We may need to find you emergency care. There are plenty of families prepared to help. I'll do what I can to find the best match. It may not be ideal, but we haven't had much notice.'

The lady on the chair looked down at the form. She pulled gently at my pen.

'Right. That's all done. I'm afraid now we'll just have to wait and see.'

I see my mother's head poking through the forms. She is singing louder now. Her mouth is moving fast. Her lips are shining. A gust of wind lifts her up and my mother takes off. Her pink balloon drifts through the white clouds.

Up, up and away, in my beautiful balloon
The world's a nicer place, in my beautiful balloon …
For we can fly, we can fly, we can fly

34

A WINTER'S TALE

Mum always wanted to be a teacher. I think she thought that if anyone can – and if prime ministers can't – then teachers can change the world. For Mum, a teacher was a middle-aged woman who wore tweed skirts and scrimped and saved to pay for her holiday in Italy. In Italy she would go and see Michelangelo. Michelangelo was the best artist in the world, Mum said, and one day she would take us to Florence to see his very special *David*.

Mum was very particular about teachers. Teachers, she thought, were like creaky old chairs that had sat around for a long time. Good teachers were valuable antiques. You put a good price tag on them. Teachers shouldn't go cheap.

Mum wouldn't have thought Dave was a good teacher, Dave, the drama teacher at Colwood, who lived somewhere near Brighton, over the hills and far away. Mum would have hated that fact, because Brighton, she said, was queer.

Queer: something unusual, odd, funny, or strange; something coming at you from a peculiar angle. It's true that Dave *was* queer. He wore bright shirts and bangles, and he leapt about a lot. But Dave was tweedy too. For one thing, he loved Shakespeare.

'Poetry in action,' Dave said. 'That's Shakespeare. Poetry that makes things happen. Strange and magical things, queer things. Now listen! This will take *five minutes*. Then you can go and get your food. But I want to tell you a story … A Winter's Tale.' Dave cleared his throat. 'King Leontes lives in Sicilia with his wife Hermione and his son Mamillius.'

'Boring, Dave, boring! We don't want to hear about fucking kings and queens.'

'Shut up, Darren, you're not bleedin' five. Listen to Dave!' That was Gary Sharp. It was always Gary Sharp or Darren Black. 'You've the attention of a gnat,' Mum said. 'A very small gnat.'

Dave cleared his throat and began. 'One day King Leontes receives a visit from his old friend Polixenes, king of Bohemia. They haven't seen one another for years. The two friends are getting on famously, one thing leads to another, and Polixenes ends up staying for longer than expected. Months go by. Months and months.'

'Freeloader!'

'Thank you, Gary. Friendship isn't always an opportunity to make a buck … but after nine months Polixenes decides that it really is time he went home. He's overstayed his welcome.'

'Fucking right he has!'

'Shhh!'

'Leontes is downcast at the thought of his friend leaving, so his wife, Hermione, tries her best to persuade him to stay.

Polixenes is duly persuaded – Hermione does a good job of convincing – but strangely, Polixenes deciding to stay on makes Leontes suspicious. Then, soon after, with no reason at all, he begins to suspect that his wife is having an affair with his old friend.'

'He should keep his dick to himself!'

'Gross, Gary. You're so gross!'

'Shut up, Trace. The only gross thing here is you.'

'Thank you, Gary! Well, things start to get out of control. Before long, Leontes instructs one of his lords, Camillo, to poison his old friend.'

'Just knife him!'

'Shut up, Darren!'

'Leontes is determined to have someone killed. He starts to scheme like a madman. But Polixenes manages to escape, so Leontes turns on his wife. He throws her into prison, which, considering she's now pregnant with his next child, is particularly cruel.'

'Wanker! He's the one who should be in prison!'

'Still, despite a lot of pleading from Hermione's friend Paulina, Leontes is unmovable.'

'Fuckin' off his rocker.'

'I couldn't put it better myself, Gary. Yes. He's off his rocker. Meanwhile, Hermione gives birth to a baby girl called Perdita. But tragically, soon after Perdita is born, Leontes' son dies and Hermione drops down dead.'

'Fuckin' hell, Dave, who the fuck's gonna believe in all these fuckin' dead bodies? I mean, *who the fuck* …?'

'Well, there lies the problem with tragedy, Darren. The play has suddenly become a tragedy, in a matter of a few scenes. Tragedy comes out of nowhere. It's beyond belief.'

'Yeah, well how do you expect *us* to believe this fuckin' stuff?'

'It's a fairy tale, Darren. I don't think anyone expects us to believe it. Listen. Leontes has made a fool of himself, lost his cool. He's made a mess of things, a bloody mess. In fact, as soon as Hermione is dead he begins to regret his decisions.'

'Twat.'

'Thank you, Gary. I don't entirely disagree.'

'Yeah, well, speed up the story, Dave! Get a move on!'

'Yeah, Dave. We haven't got all day. I'm starvin'.'

'OK. So Perdita, the daughter who survives her dead mother, Hermione, is carried off secretly by Paulina's husband, a man called Antigonus. Antigonus and Paulina are the fairy godparents of the play. It's because of them that Perdita survives. They're the good fairies.'

'I knew there'd be some fuckin' fairies showing up sometime soon. Fuckin' fairies! Dave, this is a joke!'

'Well, perhaps it is, Darren. Perhaps it's all a joke on us, the audience. If it's a joke, let's enjoy it. So Perdita is carried off to a place called Bohemia and there she becomes part of an entirely different life, a rural life, a life of shepherds and sheep and milkmaids.'

'Sounds like a fuckin' boring life to me, Dave.'

'Thank you, Gary. Now, back to Perdita. There's a young shepherd boy who falls for her. His name is Florizel, but actually he isn't a real shepherd, he's a prince in disguise. Florizel is the son of Leontes' old friend Polixenes, the king of Bohemia. OK, so Florizel falls in love with Perdita, and Perdita, remember, is a princess. After a few shenanigans, those two end up together. The play turns into a romance after all. We steer away from tragedy. The two lovers flee back to Sicilia in disguise, along with the shepherd who adopted Perdita. Now things start to move quickly. Leontes learns from the shepherd that Perdita is his lost daughter, and everyone is over the moon.'

'Fuckin' losers.'

'So, the final scene is the most extraordinary in the play, the most dramatic. Everyone goes to Paulina's house – remember her, the loyal friend of dead Hermione? So they all troop off to her house to go and look at a statue of Hermione in the chapel that Leontes has had made in her memory.'

'What do you want a fuckin' statue of your fuckin' wife for?'

'So, wait for this – as they're all standing around the statue, it begins to move. Hermione comes back to life. *Ta-da!* And there you have it: the queen comes back to life, Leontes and Hermione are together again, and Paulina is engaged to Camillo. Florizel and Perdita, of course, are going to get married. Happily ever after. *The End.*'

'What fuckin' moron is gonna believe she's been standing around for fuckin' years pretending to be a statue? Shakespeare's fuckin' stupid, Dave.'

'Yeah. "Hello, I'm" – what's-her-name? – "Herpes, and I've been hanging about for … err … fifteen years waiting for you to show up." What kind of moron stands around waiting for his wife for fifteen fuckin' years? That's fucked up, Dave, *really fucked up*!'

35

THE GREAT GIG IN THE SKY

A few weeks later we started to put on the play. Dave let Darren and Gary help him with the casting, which now I think about it was a pretty bold move.

'Who's gonna play the fuckin' dumb-arse queen who stands around acting dead then, Dave? We should ask Trace! She'll let us do anything to her. She don't care, right Trace?'

Darren was right. Tracy Stone (not my Trace, but a different Trace) let us cover her with white sheets and talcum powder and put her under lights. She didn't care, because Tracy Stone never did anything but blink.

'OK Trace, now's your moment. Move, girl. Put up your arms and wave them about. Imagine you're Jesus, fuckin' Jesus who's just heard he's been invited to a party for about the *first fuckin' time in his life*. "Woo-hoo, I'm Jesus, and I'm gonna *fuckin' par-tee … yeah!*" *Move your arms, Trace, move your fuckin' arms so we know you're coming to life! You're a person now, a real fucking person! Not just a stoner! Wave, Trace, wave!'* And Tracy Stone waved.

I played Perdita. That was Dave's idea. Perdita is the lost daughter of the king and queen and she knows about flowers.

I was never going to be a shepherd, was I? And none of the boys wanted to say these lines:

… Daffodils
That come before the swallow dares
and take the winds of March with beauty …
Pale primroses that die unmarried …

'That's just gay. What sort of guy would put up with all that fuckin' flower talk?'

'A shepherd,' Dave said.

'But he isn't a shepherd, is he? That's the fuckin' point, Dave. He's just poncin' around in a big white shirt. He looks like he's off to meet his boyfriend at the fuckin' pier. I mean, who the fuck is called "Florizel", unless they're a fuckin' pansy?'

'In the seventeenth century, flowers were the language of love and affection. If you wanted to say something, you said it with flowers,' said Dave. 'Shakespeare says a lot about flowers. Flowers were also symbols of power and status. You didn't need to be gay to think about flowers.'

'Yeah, well Shakespeare was probably gay too.'

Simon, who looked more like a girl than a boy, played Florizel, who loves Perdita. He wore a white shirt unbuttoned to show off his skinny neck and his tiny column of a chest. Dave made out that Simon was the perfect build for a boy actor in Shakespeare's time, because girls' parts were played by boys back then. Simon, who didn't mind handling plastic flowers. Simon, who found himself with flowers stuffed down the back of his trousers or the front of his shirt. Simon, who suffered it all because he looked more like a girl than a boy.

But there were parts for boys too. Dave made sure of that. In the middle of the play there's a sheep-shearing scene. Dave covered several of the boys with old rugs and mats and they crawled about bleating, knocking their bums and heads together like bumper cars. Then Dave came along and whipped off the towels, which meant they had to get up from the floor and go backstage and stop bleating.

'Sheep all sheared! Backstage please! Backstage, boys. Now!'

'Dave, we've still got loads and loads of fucking fur to get off. Look at Simon – we haven't even started on him yet. Simon, you sheep-shagger, get that fucking fleece off you. We want to see what you've got underneath! Show us your sheep, Simon, show us your sheep!'

'OK, we'll cancel the play and we'll go back to the class-room. This scene should only take a minute, not twenty-five. We need to get on to the end of the play, back to Sicilia where we can wrap things up. In the theatre you've got to keep things moving, you've got to get to the climax, the big revelation, the back-together moment. That's what the audience is waiting for. You can't spend twenty-five minutes shearing sheep, for Pete's sake.'

The play ended with Hermione standing in the middle of the dining hall with five boys pointing at her, calling her names. White lights shone on her pale face, making her blink. She looked lost and confused, but not unhappy, because Tracy Stone was always on drugs.

'Trace, if we were playing musical statues, you'd have lost with that blink.'

'Yeah, Trace, you're out. We win. We know you're not a fucking statue, all right?'

'Shh,' said Dave. 'Keep it quiet for a moment. Keep it quiet, keep it still … musical statues, remember, we're all play-ing a game of musical statues. The winner gets £5 extra spend-ing money this week. Hold it still just for a moment … just for a moment!'

And suddenly, from behind the closed canteen shutters we heard the sound of a woman wailing, a sound growing louder and louder, so loud I thought the shutters would break. We all turned around to look.

'Caterwauling,' said Dave. 'The sound of female grief … Pink Floyd, "The Great Gig in the Sky". You won't get a better representation of grief than that. *Rock Heaven*, that is. *Rock Heaven!*'

The woman's voice moved higher and higher, up towards the ceiling. 'Up, up and aw-wayyyyy. Wa-ah-wa-ah-wa-ah-wa-ah-wa-ah, wa-ah wa-ahhhh!'

I heard Dave's voice piercing through the wailing. 'Remember, this is Hermione, descending from Heaven, tell-ing her tale of grief and woe. Sing it out, girl, *sing it out!*'

'She sounds like her fuckin' cat just died,' said Darren. 'She sounds like a fat black woman whose cat's just been run over by a fat white bloke and he's really pleased and she's really fuckin' not.'

'Not just her cat, Darren – her life, her daughter, her husband, her marriage, her kingdom, her country, everything she's always known – the whole of her reality. Perhaps her cat too, but not *just* her cat!'

36

THE END

What's the difference between laughter and tears? They're very close. I think it depends a lot upon your character, whether you laugh or cry. Some people like moping about. Others wouldn't be seen dead near a tear. I don't know what makes you a laughing or a crying sort of person. Sad things happen to everyone. Speak for yourself, but I'm a laughing sort of person.

Miss Marple would never have been caught crying. No one in the Miss Marple stories cries much, except perhaps the maids – Gladys and Edna and Mary and Rose and Mabel, girls with names like that. Miss Marple isn't the sort of woman to indulge in tears. There's too much else going on: the mystery, figuring things out. Miss Marple doesn't have time for Madames or Mopers.

'Madame Mope', John Reed calls Jane Eyre. 'Madame Mope' behind the velvet curtains. Jane Eyre isn't a moper. She's a reader, a detective. But John Reed wouldn't get that. He's a hitter, a thumper, a lager lout, a moaner, a cry-baby. John Reed wouldn't care for mystery. Mystery takes courage, a bit of thinking things out. It takes some living with, because mystery is hard to bear.

Mystery depends upon what sort of prayers you say, and prayers are part of the mystery. You want answers, but they never come. The mystery just carries on. And that is definitely, without a flicker or a shadow of a doubt or a lift of an eyebrow, what we want. No matter whether we laugh or cry or what we might pretend to say.

People go on about wanting the truth. Verity. But no one really wants Verity. That's why she remains dead and buried, her body at the bottom of the garden, covered in pretty pink flowers. No, Verity works better as a memory, a sweet idea. *Pink polygonum, pink and going numb, or dumb, in several different ways, depending on how good you are at covering things up, your face going pink year after year when her name is mentioned, The Woman Upstairs, The Mad Woman in the Attic, Sue, Sweet Polygonum Sue, Sue who turns in her grave in many different ways, depending on the story you tell and how you wish to remember her, and then Him, who came before her, and all the others, in their bright pink and purple weeds. It all depends on what is about to be said, and what has already been said, in your silent conversation of prayers on the stairs.*

The conversation of prayers about to be said
By the child going to bed and the man on the stairs
Who climbs to his dying love in her high room,
The one not caring to whom in his sleep he will move
And the other full of tears that she will be dead,

Turns in the dark on the sound they know will arise
Into the answering skies from the green ground,
From the man on the stairs and the child by his bed.
The sound about to be said in the two prayers
For the sleep in a safe land and the love who dies

Will be the same grief flying.

———————

Mum's favourite poet was Dylan Thomas. Dylan Thomas was Welsh and drank a lot. I don't know much about alcohol except that the men next door at the Rotary drink it every day after work, and then Saturday and Sunday too, which is why they cause so much trouble.

Drink causes trouble. But drink can also cause poetry. At least it does for Dylan Thomas, because he has a lilt in his voice. Drink makes it so, the lilt I mean. Drink makes you tilty and lilty. Drink lifts you up and carries you away.

Dylan Thomas has a *definite lilt* in his voice, Mum says. 'Lilt' means he lifts the words up at the end. He flies off, over the hills and far away, over the bare and windy Welsh hills.

In Wales there are lots of hills. Wales is mostly made of hills, hills and sheep and then fog and farmers. I don't know if Dylan Thomas lived on a farm. I think he might have. Dylan Thomas lived on a farm and spent most of his child-hood running around the hills lilting. He lilted from his feet to his nose to his hair. Everywhere he went he was lilting.

Vicars lilt. That's how they get people to listen. Leonard lilts – Leonard the vicar, Greta's husband, that is. Vicars especially lilt on Sundays.

If you are religious you lilt. Mum thought that Dylan Thomas was religious, and that's why she liked him. Dylan Thomas may not go to church but he writes poems like prayers.

If you want to be a poet you have to know how to pray. Poets pray hard. They pray so hard that words fall out of their eyes like tears. Words fall down onto the hills until the rain soaks them up, and then they have to start again.

'A poem is a conversation in prayer,' Mum said. I didn't quite know what she meant, but I think she meant that she liked poems to sound like prayers. When you write a poem, really you are praying.

'A conversation of prayer about to be said by the man in his room and the child on the stairs.'

No, that's not right.

'The conversation of prayer about to be said by the man on the stairs and the child going to bed, the one not caring to whom he will move in his sleep turns on the quick and the dead.'

———

People move towards ghosts in their sleep. After David died, I stood in the hallway and waited for Mum to come out of her room and down the stair – there is just one small step down – down towards the kitchen. But she never came. Not once, not ever. I asked Maze why, and she said that Mum was saying her prayers and that prayers take a long time if you do it properly.

But I think Mum was saying her Dylan Thomas poem, because it was her favourite and because it brought her comfort. Dylan Thomas, that is.

After David died, Mum was waiting a long time for the man to climb up the stairs to her high room. She was waiting for God to come upstairs. Mum was waiting for God to turn the final corner of the stairs, the difficult corner, the corner that nearly tilted you sideways and sent you back down again. Mum was waiting for the man who was God to knock on her door and come in.

She knew He would. She knew, she knew, she knew. God would come through the door with an armful of roses and in the middle of the roses would be the gurgling child in his white cotton nappy. David, king of Israel. David, king of the Jews. Sweet Davy. David who gurgles and gurgles and smiles.

And the man with the child in his arms would carry the lilt in his voice right to the final turn, the man who will not care to whom in his sleep he will move, because he knew already. To Mum. To Heaven. To David. Always and always and forever. Amen.

AFTERWORD

I don't ever remember seeing my mother holding a book. All the reading she did happened before I was born. Books take up a lot of time, and you have to be still and silent as a statue, Mum said, to get really stuck in. She didn't have time with us lot under her feet. Fat lot of good a book would do her with those nappies to change.

But Mum had words stored up: she had Shakespeare and Hugh Walpole; she had Dylan Thomas – who she forgave for being Welsh, because of his lilt. Somewhere deep inside, Mum had saved some poetry. And this is what kept her going, thorough bush, thorough brier, thorough flood, thorough fire. *After all this.*

It was Mum who first sent me to the library. I was six and I learned the way through the woods to the building with the fading green spire. At the library I found the Milly-Molly-Mandy books and Agatha Christie and then *Jane Eyre*. And I sat on the floor of the children's library and read and read and nobody back home knew I was there. I read sitting on a shiny wooden floor that squeaked whenever I moved. I learned to sit still and silent as a statue so I could read as much as I could before leaving. Because you were only allowed five books, and five books would last me five days. I would have to come back on Saturday, late morning, after my chores. And that's how reading was, for years.

Going to the library meant leaving my granite-grey house on Granville Road by the sea and walking to the edge of Lobs Wood. Lobs Wood was where the dogwalkers went in the daytime. Lobs Wood was where murderers buried bodies at nightfall. I sat in Lobs Wood with Greta Clementine and her husband and traced with my finger around the lines and squares of their vicarage home. I imagined murderers from St Mary Mead coming through the front-room window and dragging dead bodies there. I imagined Miss Marple peeking through her window before picking up the phone to Dolly Bantry.

In Lobs Wood I studied diagrams of houses I longed to live in; houses where the chances of a murder happening were guaranteed. Absolutely bet your bottom dollar, without a doubt. Someone would be knocked off before tea.

I read mostly outdoors because there was no room in our house for quiet reading. I read sitting on a wooden stump beneath a canopy of trees. I read inside a white circle of puffy cow parsley. I read blowing the heads off the dandelions. And when I read *Jane Eyre* I imagined I was sitting with Helen Burns, her clever friend, in the garden of Lowood School; Helen, whose reading age was far ahead of mine, but I would catch up soon, I told myself, and I turned to the pale-faced girl with her head bent towards the ground.

'Is your book interesting?' I asked. I had already decided that I would ask to borrow it the minute she put it down.

'I like it,' she answered after a pause of a second or two, during which time she examined me.

'What's it about?' I continued. I hardly knew how I dared ask this question, but something about her struck a chord in me, a note of sympathy. I looked at the title written along the spine and I could make out 'Rass-e-las'. Rass and Lass. Rasse-Lassie. It was a strange name, more like a dog's than a person's, a name from far away.

'You may look at it,' said the pale girl, lifting her head. 'Miss Temple gave it to me. She says it is a book for those in search of happiness.'

Then she looked straight at me and I knew at once she was my fairy-friend.

———————

But fairies can suddenly vanish. They disappear like sprites in the night. One night, Helen Burns dies of consumption; she catches a high fever and dies in her dear friend's arms. Jane loses Helen, but she keeps her reading. She preserves her friend in words. Jane turns the page and Helen is there, drawing out the words.

———————

Jane Eyre likes to draw. She turns words into pictures. Mr Rochester of Thornfield Hall asks to see her pictures. They puzzle and intrigue him. He knows they come from a strange world, a world of fairies and genies, goblins and sprites. Jane Eyre is a strange creature. Hers is a world of moonlight and scudding clouds, of tall dark trees and towers. He longs to be part of this world. Given half the chance Mr Rochester would like to be a fairy too.

Because Jane Eyre has imagination, and imagination radically alters things. It changes outlooks and aspects, of people and places, moods and feelings, even the very end of things, who marries who. Imagination can turn your grey house into a bower of flowers. But once you let it in, it is bound to turn you out of doors. Imagination will soon send you packing into the wide green world.

In the public library of my small seaside town I began to find my way into the world. I hadn't read *Rasselas* yet, but years later I did.

And when I did, the picture of Jane Eyre in the garden of Lowood came rushing back to me; and close behind her, another picture, of a pale-faced girl on a tree stump in Lobs Wood poised to ask her question.

'What are you reading? May I see?'

ACKNOWLEDGEMENTS

It was my grandmother who taught me to read and pay attention to words, so this book begins with her. It was my mother who taught me to love poetry and the sound of words. Much of this book comes from her singing voice.

This book exists because of teachers: Mr Harding of Littlehampton Community College who brought me to Wordsworth in a mouldy hut on the edge of a playing field. Vicky Craver of Brighton and Hove Sixth Form College, and her colleague Margaret Blythe, who taught me Shakespeare and Byron and allowed me to read beyond the syllabus. I have never forgotten reading *Clarissa* with you.

And then Dave, who brought Shakespeare alive during difficult times; Dave who brought me books when I had few and who showed me what it was to be an Autolycus.

Finally, Stephen Boyd, who taught me at St Andrews University, and whose life was cut short. You brought me the linguistic playfulness of Joyce and then Dante's *La Vita Nuova* which you said I must read, and I did. *Élan vital*, you said in your letter, I must always keep my *élan vital*.

Many people have encouraged and shaped the writing of this book. I owe a great deal to the students and young people I have taught; this book is for them. I dedicate the final chapter to Noreen Masud, whose journey into voice I have been privileged to share. Noreen, I will never forget teaching you the poetry of Dylan Thomas at Jesus College in your first year: 'The force that through the green fuse drives the flower.' Your vivid literary imagination and forceful intellect have been a source of inspiration. You have taught me a lot. Thank you.

I am fortunate to have nurturing literary friends. I want to thank Dennis Harrison, Ben Morgan, Will May, Thalia Suzuma, Sunetra Gupta, Laura Ashby, John Hood, Kelsey Finkel, Stephen Pickles, Charlie Lee-Potter, Adam Swift and Tom MacFaul especially for encouraging me to write this book and for reading it during its lumpen days. Dennis, I followed your instructions. Tom, I listened to your advice. Will, you are the best reader anyone could ask for: thank you.

Especial thanks to Tracy Brain, my literary seamstress, and dear, encouraging friend and sister. Thank you for showing me what female kinship can be. And thank you to Alexandra Lewis for her loyal humour and wise compassion. You are a true Athena.

Thank you again to Dennis and the Albion Beatnik Bookshop for offering me somewhere to read and write.

Thank you also to 'Ticci' Randall and Sally Turner too for being kind early readers, and to Emma Hagestadt for her sensitive reading and rallying of my sentences and for her consistent warmth as a reader. Thank you to Frankie

Henderson, Lucie Richter-Mahr and Jessica Tomey for being loyal girl-readers and advisers.

Many thanks to Robert Lacey for offering such consistently fine judgement during the final phases of editing. Thank you for all your patience and care.

Thank you to Agatha Christie Limited for granting permission to use material, and especially to Annabelle Mannix for her sensitive handling of my young relationship to Miss Marple. My eight-year-old self is very grateful.

I owe a lot to my dear friend and literary sister Paula Byrne, who has been such a champion of my lived and creative choices. 'I am no bird; and no net ensnares me; I am a free human being with an independent will' (*Jane Eyre*). You have shown me this. I will never forget what you have done to help me and I always be grateful.

Thank you to my editor Arabella Pike, who has been so generous, supportive and trusting of my methods. Thank you for allowing me to follow my intuition and for your wisdom, knowledge and kind guidance. Thank you for sharing books with me. You are a writer's true champion.

Thank you also to Sarah Chalfant of the Wylie Agency for her commitment to my work and progress in the world. I am a young pilgrim, so thank you Sarah for your loyalty and faith in me. Thank you too to Alba Ziegler-Bailey for your warmth and kind intelligence and your extraordinary gift for listening.

Thank you too to dear friends who have lived with this project for a long time: Nasir Khan, Marc Lafrance, Julie

Sutherland, Monika Class, Andrew Blades, Matt Hill, Nadia Hilliard, Ray Hilliard, Nigel Bowles, Gerard Whyte, Christy Edwall, Angie Johnson, Alexandra Harris, Amy Winchester, John Warriner, Una Eve. Thank you to Jemima Hunt for being an early reader and supporter of this book.

I want to thank my former student and friend Andrew Hay for sharing Agatha Christie with me. Andrew, I will always remember you singing the theme tune to the Margaret Rutherford versions. 'Very jaunty,' you said. Andrew, you are very missed. Rest in Peace.

Thank you to Suzie Hanna for all the years we have shared film and poetry together; your imagination and filmic methods are part of this book. I owe you a lot.

Thank you to Liz Marchbank for providing me with an essential part of my story. Most of all, thank you for being Somebody's Mother.

Thank you to Rosemary and Eric Thompson, and Suzie, Richard and Catalina for all your love and support; thank you for including me in your family.

Thank you to my brothers for your continued love and support; I am so glad to have you still.

Thank you to West Sussex County Council Social Services and their social workers for 'redoing the paperwork'; and for supporting me financially during my first years at university.

Finally, I want to thank the Littlehampton Town Library for providing me with a free education from the ages of five to fifteen. Without those books I could never have found my way past the curtains.